The modesty of this book is inversely proportional to its accomplishment: judicious, clear, winsome, thorough, disciplined, accessible, and articulate. Gerald Bray writes in the spirit of J. I. Packer and John Stott and has gifted the church with an unrivaled brief introduction to Anglicanism. Deo gratias!

Mark Bowald
professor of theology,
Grace Theological Seminary

Gerald Bray's helpful survey of the history and historic formularies of the Anglican tradition succeeds, on the one hand, in capturing the many-splendored character of Anglicanism, while demonstrating on the other that it is "Reformed Catholicism"—a Reformation church within the ancient Catholic tradition.

Joel Scandrett
assistant professor of theology
at Trinity School for Ministry;
editor of *To Be a Christian: An Anglican Catechism*

ANGLICANISM

A Reformed Catholic Tradition

ANGLICANISM

A Reformed Catholic Tradition

Gerald Bray

LEXHAM PRESS

Anglicanism: A Reformed Catholic Tradition

Copyright 2021 Gerald Bray

Lexham Press, 1313 Commercial St., Bellingham, WA 98225
LexhamPress.com

Print ISBN 9781683594369
Digital ISBN 9781683594376
Library of Congress Control Number 2020947198

Lexham Editorial: Todd Hains, Matthew Boffey, Abigail Stocker, Jessi Strong
Cover Design: Peter Park
Interior Design: Sarah Vaughan

*To the Anglican students at Beeson Divinity School
who are bearing witness to this tradition in
an ecumenical and evangelical context*

Contents

What is Anglicanism?

Anglicanism as we think of it today is essentially a nineteenth-century invention. The elements that make it up are much older than that, of course, but it was only from the 1830s or so that the particular configuration that Christianity assumed in the post-Reformation Church of England and its sister churches came to be regarded as something unique. Before that time, most people assumed that the Church of England was a Protestant body that had separated from Rome in the sixteenth century along with several other churches in Northern Europe. Everyone knew that the details of the separation were unusual, and that political factors had played as much of a role as theological ones, but these secondary matters did not affect the basic principle. The English church happened to have preserved a number of medieval features, like a territorial episcopate with cathedrals that continued to function much as they had before the Reformation. This gave it a certain traditional-ist feel, which might look to Protestants like remnants of Roman Catholicism, but this was more in appearance than in reality. Almost all members of the Church of England saw themselves as Protestants and regarded Rome with varying degrees of enmity.

It was only when secularism began to take hold, and the bonds of church and state started to weaken, that people began to ask about the nature of the Church of England. Was it a Protestant church with distinctive characteristics or a Catholic church no longer in communion with Rome? That, in turn, raised the question of what catholicity is. Rome was quite clear that to be Catholic meant being in communion with the Holy See and accepting the pope as head of the church on earth, the vicar of Christ. English churchmen could not agree with that, and some of them pointed to the Eastern Orthodox churches, which were just as ancient as Rome but had not been in communion with it for eight hundred years. Could the Church of England claim a similar kind of non-Roman catholicity? Those who thought that it could were the first to use the term "Anglicanism."

For these first self-conscious Anglicans, Protestantism and the Reformation were a problem. Their impact on the Church of England could hardly be denied altogether, but the theorists of Anglicanism tended to minimize their significance. They agreed that the late medieval church needed reforming, but they claimed that in England, existing abuses were corrected but no new doctrines or practices were introduced. Anglicanism was thus understood to be a kind of reformed Catholicism, better than what Rome had to offer, but not really different from what had gone before. In order to substantiate that argument, they were forced to overlook much of what happened in the sixteenth century and restrict the word Anglican to those who opposed the Puritans, whom they regarded as an alien import into the English church. As they saw it, the Puritans were eventually defeated and the Church of England was able to express its true Anglican identity.

This interpretation of English church history might have been dismissed as eccentric had it not coincided with another development that made it convenient to promote Anglicanism as a distinct form of Christianity. This was the expansion of English Christianity to other parts of the world, which took different forms. Ireland and even Scotland (for a while) had national churches that were in communion with the Church of England, though they did not refer to themselves as "Anglican" until modern times because they did not see themselves as being English. Colonial settlers took the English church to North America, Australasia, and other parts of the world, and at first were quite happy, even determined, to call themselves "English." But as they became independent of the mother country some other designation was called for and eventually "Anglican" met this need. Beyond the settler churches, members of the Church of England planted missions across the globe, whose converts were in no sense "English." For them it was pointless to try to re-create the Church of England in Africa or Asia, but they could not easily deny their origins. Was it possible to establish local churches in other countries that would look like the mother Church of England and be in communion with it? Could these churches be Anglican without being English?

These questions have been addressed and answered in different ways. In some places, like India, Anglican missions have joined in with other Protestants and created national churches of their own. Whether these churches are Anglican or not has been a matter of considerable discussion. In the ecumenical climate of our time, they are usually recognized as such, though their interdenominational origin gives them a character that is distinct from that of other Anglican churches that have not joined a wider ecumenical union. In most parts of the world, however, Anglican churches have preferred to retain their distinctiveness even to the point of refusing to join interdenominational groupings. For them, defining Anglicanism is an essential part of their identity, even though that identity may have little to do with the historical English church.

More recently, splits within the American Episcopal Church have created a situation in which breakaway groups are more likely to call themselves "Anglican" as distinct from "Episcopalian," the assumption presumably being that "Anglican" indicates a form of Episcopalianism that is more authentic, more universal, and more orthodox, but not necessarily more English. In the Church of England, by way of contrast, there are parishioners who would never describe themselves as Anglican and who may not know what the term means. They are aware that the Church of England is different from other denominations, but most of them have little idea of what Anglicanism is and are not particularly interested in finding out. Their conception of what a church should be is determined by their parish, which may or may not be typical of what exists elsewhere. Many congregants will be aware of that diversity but have chosen to worship where they do because their parish reflects what they think the church should be like. The breadth of Anglicanism may thus be something of which they are conscious but of which they disapprove for different reasons and to varying degrees. To their minds, what they do (or prefer) is what Anglicanism ought to be, and often they are quite prepared to ignore, criticize, or even condemn those who do not conform to their chosen paradigm.

Given this situation, we must accept that however "Anglicanism" is defined, it has emerged in a particular historical context, it embraces different and sometimes conflicting perspectives, and many people who subscribe to it have a narrower view of what it is (or should be) than outside observers often do. The truth is, many Anglicans find it difficult to live alongside others who claim the same denominational label but interpret it very differently, and they are often inclined to define their church in ways that implicitly, if not explicitly, exclude those who do not share their perspective. There is no easy way around this problem, and no definition of Anglicanism that will satisfy everyone. The best we can do is revisit the history, try to understand how we arrived where we are, and ask ourselves whether some theological trajectories are more consistent and more faithful to the ongoing Anglican tradition than others are.

To do this, we must begin with the origins of English Christianity and consider to what extent modern Anglicanism can be said to be in continuity with it, and then look at each of its historical phases and assess their contribution to modern Anglicanism.

THE PRE-REFORMATION
CHURCH OF ENGLAND

It is generally agreed that a distinct form of Christianity that might be called Anglican emerged out of the Protestant Reformation in the sixteenth century. But the Church of England, known in Latin as the *Ecclesia Anglicana*, had already been in existence for nearly a thousand years before that. Missions to the English had been sent from Ireland (in the north) and Rome (in the south) in the sixth century, and these fused into what became the Anglo-Saxon church. Its great chronicler was Bede (673–735), who lived and worked in the monastery of Jarrow, now a suburb of Newcastle-upon-Tyne. Anglo-Saxon and Irish missionaries were responsible for the conversion of Germany and Scandinavia to Christianity, a process that was complete by about AD 1000. By the sixteenth century, this period had largely been forgotten, apart from the names of missionary saints to whom a number of parish churches were dedicated. But after the break with Rome, there was a desire to recover the sources of English Christianity, of which modern Anglicanism has seen periodic revivals of interest, amounting in some cases to a claim that in its Irish (Celtic) dimension, the Church of England had an origin independent of the papacy. That claim was always dubious and is now generally rejected, but traces of it can still be found in some modern Anglican writers.

In 1066, William of Normandy conquered England and ushered in a new era. The Church of England's administrative structure was thoroughly reformed, and much of it survived the Reformation to become characteristic (though not definitive) of modern Anglicanism. In particular, a parish system was introduced and tithing regulated. Parish priests were appointed, and after 1215 they were given "benefices" or "livings," a source of income based on tithe revenue that was supposed to be enough to sustain them. Appointments to parishes were technically in the hands of the diocesan bishop, but very often the right of nomination belonged to local landowners, the king, or other lay people, who could present a man of their choice for the bishop to institute to the church. The man so appointed would normally be the receiver of the tithe, or "rector," a title that is still in regular use in Anglican circles today. In slightly more than a third of all English parishes, however, the right of presentation fell into the hands of various monasteries, whose abbots became the rectors. Since they could not reside on the benefice themselves, they sent substitutes, or "vicars," who performed the duties of the parish priest. Today, "rector" and "vicar" are treated as synonymous. Both terms are still in use, but neither has anything to do with ordination or ecclesiastical status. The tithe system no longer functions, but its legacy survives in the titles given to the incumbents of parishes, both in England and in the wider Anglican Communion. It is an example of how a tradition can metastasize and become fossilized within Anglicanism, even to the point of acquiring a religious significance that it did not originally have.

The medieval English church produced some outstanding scholars and theologians, but for the most part they are not usually regarded as Anglican now. Some were not even English. Anselm of Canterbury, for example, was archbishop there from 1093 to 1109 and one of the greatest theologians of all time, but he was originally from northern Italy, had been abbot of the monastery of Bec in Normandy, and probably did not speak a word of English. On the other hand, there were Englishmen who made careers in France, especially at the monastery of St. Victor in Paris. Richard and Andrew of St. Victor were leading theologians and biblical scholars in the twelfth century, as were men like Stephen Langton and Robert Grosseteste. The latter two returned to England, the first as archbishop of Canterbury and the second as bishop of Lincoln, and although their legacy is remembered in some circles, neither they nor any of their contemporaries can be called Anglican in any sense that would be meaningful today. The same must be said of William of Ockham (1287–1347), whose European reputation is beyond question but who left England fairly early on and made his career in France and Germany, where he died. These men and others like them were part of the universal *respublica Christiana*, the "Christian commonwealth," as it is sometimes called, and they cannot be said to have represented a distinctively Anglican form of Christianity.

The only medieval figure to be remembered today as a proto-Anglican is John Wycliffe or Wyclif (1328–1384). This is mainly because Wycliffe advocated the supreme authority of Holy Scripture in matters of faith, denied the doctrine of transubstantiation that undergirded late medieval teaching on the Lord's Supper, and rejected the authority of the pope. In other words, it is the apparent Protestantism of Wycliffe that makes people think of him as somehow Anglican, though he would never have thought of himself in that way. Wycliffe was the moving spirit behind the Lollards, a group who promoted Bible translation into English and provided theological training for interested lay people. The Lollards survived until the Reformation, when they merged seamlessly into the Church of England. Wycliffe and the Lollards were regarded as heroes by Jan Hus and his Bohemian Brethren, who copied their works and tried to apply similar doctrines and practices in their own country. Hus later influenced Luther, and for that reason Wycliffe came to be known as the "morning star of the Reformation." Wycliffe continues to be honored in the Anglican world as he is among Protestants more generally, but as many modern scholars have pointed out, the picture painted of him in those circles is decidedly limited and one-sided. He believed in the supreme authority of Scripture and rejected transubstantiation, but in other matters he was typical of his age and could not be called a "Reformer" in the sixteenth-century sense. Wycliffe has been an inspiration to many later Protestants, but he was not one himself and should not be understood in that way.

In the early sixteenth century, the Church of England began to feel the effects of Renaissance humanism, and the calls for reform (or modernization, as we would now call it) became louder. Monastic education gradually gave way to the universities of Oxford and Cambridge, from which the parish clergy were increasingly drawn, and the presence of Erasmus in the latter university (1511–1514) had an electrifying effect on the Church. Men like John Colet and Sir Thomas More began to press for changes, particularly in the education of priests, and Thomas Wolsey, who became archbishop of York and was the king's chief minister from 1516 to 1529, began turning monasteries into colleges in an effort to achieve this goal. None of these men can be called Anglican, and the legacy of More and Wolsey (in particular) remains contested, but in some respects they laid the foundations for the reforms that were to come. To that extent they can be regarded as forerunners of later Anglicanism, though they would certainly have rejected the Reformation had they lived to see it.

In general, it can be said that although the pre-Reformation Church of England, along with the Celtic church, plays a part in the self-consciousness of Anglicans today, it exerts relatively little influence on modern Anglican thought or practice. On the other hand, Anglicanism is deeply rooted in the Western Christianity that for a thousand years was governed from Rome. Nowadays, Anglicans usually maintain friendly relations with Roman Catholics and other Protestants. There is full communion between the Church of England and the Old Catholic Church, and also between Lutherans and Anglicans in many parts of the world. Anglicans have also tried to establish links with the different Eastern churches, like the Greek and Russian Orthodox, but Anglicanism is quite unlike those churches in its pattern of worship, form of governance, and so on. This is true even of Anglican churches in the Middle East, where Eastern Christianity is dominant, and intercommunion between them remains a distant dream.

THE LUTHERAN INFLUENCE ON EARLY ANGLICANISM

When Martin Luther (1483–1546) raised the banner of revolt in Germany, reaction in England was largely indifferent or negative. Henry VIII wrote a treatise against him (*Assertion of the Seven Sacraments*), which earned him the title Defender of the Faith from Pope Leo X (a title that his successors still bear) but did nothing to endear him to Luther. It was only in 1534, when Henry broke with the papacy because of the pope's refusal to annul his marriage, that an opening to the Lutherans became realistic as the king looked around for allies. By then, William Tyndale (1494–1536) had already gone to Germany and met Martin Luther in person—probably the first Englishman to do so, and certainly Luther's earliest English disciple. Inspired by Luther's example, Tyndale translated the New Testament and much of the Old into English, adding prefaces at the beginning of each book (as Luther had done) to explain their teaching. It was in these prefaces that Tyndale developed what would later become covenant theology, the typical Reformed way of reading the Bible as a single message from God—salvation promised in the Old Testament and realized in the New. Tyndale also wrote a number of theological tracts that were widely circulated in England and encouraged the spread of Protestant ideas.

Tyndale would not have called himself an Anglican, but he has a better claim to the designation than anyone who went before him. His beliefs and his translations laid the foundation for later Anglican theology, which can rightly be seen as having developed from his work. He never returned to England and was eventually arrested, tried, and executed for heresy in Belgium, but even as those events were playing out, ambassadors from Henry VIII were making their way to Wittenberg, hoping to iron out a common theological position. The Lutherans had already composed a confession of faith, which they had submitted to Emperor Charles V at Augsburg in 1530. This *Augsburg Confession* (*Confessio Augustana*) became the yardstick by which Protestantism was measured, and the Lutherans wanted the English to sign up to it.

That the English ambassadors could not do. This is partly because Henry VIII did not agree with much of it, and partly because no English government would submit to a foreign jurisdiction, not even in theology. The ambassadors themselves, however, were largely won over to the Lutheranism of Augsburg and did what they could to introduce it into their own proposals for an English confession of faith. The Ten Articles of 1536 managed to include a more-or-less Lutheran doctrine of justification by faith alone and expressed serious doubts about the existence of purgatory (key to the sale of indulgences against which Luther had originally protested), but on other matters, such as transubstantiation, they toed a more conservative line. Nevertheless, it is clear from the explanatory commentary on these Articles, published in 1537 as *The Institution of a Christian Man* (known to us as the "Bishops' Book" because it was endorsed by all the serving bishops in the Church), that Lutheran beliefs were making headway. But we also know that Henry VIII was not pleased with it, and when a revised version of the book appeared in 1543 (known as the King's Book), many of its more Protestant elements had been suppressed, often at his request.

During these years of apparent anti-Lutheran reaction, Thomas Cranmer (1489–1556), archbishop of Canterbury from 1533, was quietly devising a prospective confession of faith that was very close to the Augsburg Confession. It was found among his papers after his death and published as the Thirteen Articles, to which three more can be attached, making sixteen in all. Cranmer's project never came to fruition, but there is no doubt that he was moving in a more Protestant direction. He even attempted to win over Henry VIII by refuting Henry's objections to *The Institution of a Christian Man*, but largely without success. Henry was reverting to traditional Catholicism, and any moves towards Lutheranism had to be put on hold until after he died. By the time that occurred in 1547, Luther had already passed away, and the Lutheran cause in Germany was under serious strain. The English were already looking more toward the Swiss Reformers, who had carved out a theological position distinct from Luther's, and Lutheran influence on the Church of England rapidly declined after 1547.

Cranmer was assisted in his efforts to remake the Church of England by men like Hugh Latimer (1487–1555) and Nicholas Ridley (1500–1555), both of whom were great preachers. Their work was continued in the next generation by John Jewel (1522–1571), Matthew Parker (1504–1575), and Alexander Nowell (1517–1602). Parker was largely responsible for the revision of the *Thirty-nine Articles of Religion*. Jewel wrote many of the homilies in the *Second Book*. Nowell authored the catechism, which was designed to teach its principles to children over time. Taken together, the work of these men can be said to have created the structure of the post-Reformation Church of England, and therefore of classical Anglicanism as we know it today.

A MIDDLE WAY BETWEEN LUTHER AND THE SWISS REFORMERS?

In the early sixteenth century, the Swiss Confederation was still part of the Holy Roman Empire, as was Wittenberg, but it was composed of self-governing cantons that were free to devise their own forms of Protestantism. The most important of these was German-speaking Zurich, where Huldrych Zwingli (1484–1531) had introduced a reformation about the same time Luther did in Wittenberg. We may also include French-speaking Geneva, although it was not yet a member of the Swiss Confederation, which after 1541 was under the influence of John Calvin (1509–1564) and was in continual dialogue with Zurich. The English felt particularly close to Heinrich Bullinger (1501–1575), Zwingli's successor at Zurich, and he exercised considerable influence over them. Calvin also attracted attention in England, though his main impact on English theology did not come until the 1550s, after which it grew to become dominant for the rest of the sixteenth century.

The Swiss were more interested in the doctrines of church, ministry, and sacraments than Luther was, and their rejection of medieval theology was more radical than his had been. Luther had denied transubstantiation, but he continued to give a high value to the gospel sacraments of baptism and the Lord's Supper, which he regarded as efficient means of God's grace, even if he did not define this too precisely, a fact that led to controversy among his followers after he died. As for the Swiss, Bullinger and Calvin had their differences over the sacraments but were able to reach agreement in 1549 in the *Consensus Tigurinus*, and this appealed to the English more than the conservatism of Luther's followers. Following the logic of justification by faith alone, the Swiss Reformers insisted that the benefits of the sacraments came only to those who received them by faith. To some people, this meant they should be administered only to those who made a profession of faith, and it was among them that the practice of infant baptism was first questioned and abandoned.

The mainline Swiss Reformers did not draw that conclusion, however. They saw the sacraments as forms of preaching the word of God, offering the promise of salvation to those who received them in faith but without demanding a faith commitment from the recipients in advance. Thus, they were able to preserve the practice of infant baptism without having to say that all the baptized were genuine Christians. This combination suited the English perfectly. As members of a national church, they could not restrict the practice of infant baptism or prevent people from coming to Holy Communion, but they knew that those who had no faith did not receive the grace of God merely by partaking of external sacramental rites. By adopting a view similar to that of the *Consensus Tigurinus*, they could continue to minister to the entire population of England without passing judgment on them, but at the same time they could also insist that a personal commitment of faith was essential for living the Christian life. They did their best to avoid offending the more conservative Lutherans, but in the end they failed to construct a real "middle way" (*via media*) between them and the Swiss, because the Lutherans would not compromise. What we now call Anglicanism first emerged as a kind of Reformed Protestantism.

Many modern Anglicans define their church as a "middle way" between Roman Catholicism and a Calvinistic kind of Protestantism, but this is incorrect. Rome was always held at arm's length by the sixteenth-century Reformers, although they were sometimes more moderate in their criticisms of Catholicism than other Protestants were. Unlike many Lutherans and Presbyterians, for example, they refused to call the pope "Antichrist," though they regarded him as the head of a church that had fallen into error (see Article 19 of the *Articles of Religion*). But Anglican moderation in matters like these must not be misinterpreted, as some modern exponents of a "high church" tendency have done. The Church of England was firmly Protestant after the Elizabethan Settlement of 1559, and Anglicanism has remained so ever since, despite some claims to the contrary (see below).

THE FORMULARIES OF THE CHURCH OF ENGLAND

It was after the death of Henry VIII, during the short reign of his son Edward VI, that the English Reformation acquired theological substance. Because the king was a minor, control of the Church was delegated to Thomas Cranmer as archbishop, and a full-blown scheme of reform was enacted. Every church has to have a pattern of doctrine, discipline, and devotion, and the reformed Church of England was no exception. Cranmer tackled doctrine almost immediately in the *First Book of Homilies*, a series of twelve sermons outlining the main points of Protestant belief, though without calling it that. Later on, he composed a more concise set of forty-two articles, which he published shortly before the king's death in 1553. These articles were later revised and in 1563 became the *Thirty-nine Articles of Religion* that we know today. A further revision occurred in 1571, since when they have remained unaltered.

The *Thirty-nine Articles of Religion* are the Church of England's confession of faith. Some people claim that they are not systematic enough to be a true confession, but this is a judgment from hindsight based on the more detailed Westminster Confession of Faith, which was composed nearly a century later and began as a conscious attempt to improve the Thirty-nine Articles. Compared with the confessions produced before them, the Thirty-nine Articles are more comprehensive and systematic than the Augsburg Confession on which they were broadly modelled, and generations of Anglican theologians have based their exposition of Anglicanism on them. Some of the articles, like the one on excommunication (33), are no longer applicable in their original sense, and others, like the one on the need to worship in the vernacular (24), seem to be unnecessary nowadays, but on the whole they have stood the test of time. It is true that they were never intended to be a complete statement of Anglican doctrine and, on some subjects, have to be supplemented from other sources, but that does not detract from their value. The sum total of Anglican theology may be more than the Articles, but it is not less.

The Articles themselves begin with a reaffirmation of classical Christian doctrine, going back to the early church period, and on many subjects (eschatology, for example) Anglicans have usually relied on the consensus of the pre-Reformation period for guidance. The English Reformers either did not regard subjects like that as controversial, or, if they did, the subjects were not sufficiently central to their concerns to necessitate taking a particular position concerning them. As a result, modern Anglicans generally accept the essentially amillenarian approach developed by Augustine of Hippo in his great *City of God*, but this is seldom if ever central to Anglican theological interests, and if someone prefers another interpretation, there is nothing to stop him or her from putting it forward. The Church is not committed either to accepting or to rejecting it—it becomes one possibility among others that have been put forward by Anglicans but that have not been adopted by the Church as definitive of its position.

A similar thing can be said about the atoning work of Christ. Different theories have circulated in the Church over time, and some are clearly associated with particular groups within it. Evangelical Anglicans, for example, believe that on the cross Jesus took our place and paid the price for our sins. This is the penal substitutionary theory of the atonement, and it seems to come closest to what the New Testament teaches. But there have been other theories, like the satisfaction theory of Anselm of Canterbury, according to which Christ paid the price for every human sin, even if only some actually benefit from that. There is also the exemplary theory, which regards Christ as an example of suffering rather than as our substitute, though this theory suffers from the defect of turning Jesus into the first Christian and expecting us to atone for our own sins. In recent times, there has even been a theory generally known as *Christus Victor*, named after a well-known book of the same name by the Swedish Lutheran theologian Gustav Aulén (1879–1977).

According to him, Christ fought the powers of sin and death represented by Satan and hell and achieved a cosmic redemption that is then applied to individuals.

Theologians debate the merits of these different theories, and some ignore the problem altogether, but they are free to do so within the parameters of Anglican theology because there has never been a definitive statement that would insist on one (or more) of these interpretations to the exclusion of the others. However, that does not mean that particular Anglicans do not hold strong views on the subject or regard it as peripheral to their theology. For evangelical Anglicans, penal substitutionary atonement is central to the gospel, and they do not accept any alternative to it. But at the same time, they cannot unchurch other Anglicans who disagree with them, nor can those Anglicans excommunicate evangelicals for holding to their position. Men like Leon Morris (1914–2006) and John Stott (1921–2011) were both Anglican evangelicals who wrote important works on the subject, but as with writers on eschatology, they were Anglicans with a particular theology that is shared by many outside the confines of the Anglican Communion, not exponents of an "Anglican theology" that would be recognized as such by those from other traditions. Much the same would have to be said of any other Anglicans writing about the atonement, whatever position they might take and however strongly they might insist on it. Whether we like it or not, on subjects as important as these, there is no specifically Anglican theology. Anglicans can (and sometimes do) express widely divergent views on such matters, and they can do so freely because there is nothing in the Anglican tradition to suggest that they ought to follow one doctrinal approach as opposed to any others.

Bearing this in mind, what other sources are important for the study of Anglican theology? Article 35 points to the *Homilies*, and in particular to the *Second Book*, which was produced in 1563 and revised in 1571, as more detailed explanations of their meaning, and so they should be studied as Anglican doctrine alongside the Articles. Article 36 commends the Ordinal, or form of ordination for bishops, priests, and deacons, which was composed in 1550 and is normally annexed to the *Book of Common Prayer*. Taken together, these three documents constitute the doctrinal foundation of Anglicanism.

The *Book of Common Prayer* represents the devotional pillar of the Church, and many Anglicans believe that it is also a principal source of its doctrine. One of the difficulties with that viewpoint is that there are several books of "Common Prayer," and it is not always clear which one is being referred to. Historically speaking, the first *Book of Common Prayer* appeared in 1549 and is regarded by some people as foundational for the subsequent tradition. However, most scholars believe that it was merely a preparatory volume for the second *Book of Common Prayer*, which came out in 1552. It is this second book that is the template for the 1559, 1604, and 1662 editions, the last of which remains the official liturgy of the Church of England.

The 1549 Prayer Book tradition was continued in the 1637 Scottish Book (to which the Scots themselves furiously objected) and in the American Prayer Book of 1786, which was a conscious attempt by the Episcopal Church to distance itself from England after the American Revolution. In modern times, liturgical revision has produced any number of Prayer Books, which enjoy varying degrees of authority and acceptance in the different provinces of the Anglican

Communion. Because of this, there is now no longer any real unity of worship among Anglicans, though theologians tend to default to the 1662 Book when an authoritative liturgy is sought. That approach has been strengthened in recent years as conflicts within the Anglican world have led theologians and liturgists to seek common ground, and it is hard to see how any Prayer Book could now exert the influence (or claim the authority) of the 1662 version.

The idea that the Prayer Book counts as a source of doctrine reflects a tradition that can be traced back to Prosper of Aquitaine in the fifth century, because it was he who produced the maxim *lex orandi lex credendi* ("the law of praying is the law of believing"). This has been interpreted by some Anglicans to mean that the Prayer Book is the basis for interpreting the other Anglican formularies, though as a matter of historical fact it is the other way around. Archbishop Cranmer composed his two Prayer Books in order to reflect his doctrine, a point that was brought out even by a hostile critic like Gregory Dix, author of *The Shape of the Liturgy*, a book that (for better or worse) has influenced much of Anglican liturgical revision in the past century. That doctrine is summarized in the Thirty-nine Articles and sometimes expounded more fully in the *Homilies*, which serve as guides and interpreters of the meaning of the words of the liturgy.

Where the sixteenth-century Church of England differed most from other Reformed Protestants was in its internal discipline, or relative lack thereof. Most Reformed churches abolished the medieval canon law inherited from Rome and produced forms of church government that they claimed to derive from the Bible. The Church of England originally intended to follow suit, but the plans made by Archbishop Cranmer for disciplinary reform were shelved, and no real progress was made. Medieval canon law remained in force (as it still does, to some extent), and every attempt to create a systematic discipline was frustrated, mainly by the Crown, which feared losing control of the Church. It was this failure that led to the rise of Puritanism and the eventual division of the Church when it proved impossible to agree on a form of discipline acceptable to all. Much of what now appears as distinctive about Anglicanism can be traced back to this failure of disciplinary reform in the sixteenth century. Had that been carried out as Cranmer and his colleagues intended, classical (and presumably also modern) Anglicanism would have looked more Protestant than it does. But that should not be allowed to obscure the Reformed character of the Church's official doctrine and classical liturgy, which remain more closely allied with Geneva than with either Wittenberg or Rome.

A CONTESTED LEGACY

After the adoption of the Thirty-nine Articles in their current form (1571), the Church of England ceased to make official doctrinal statements. This was not because its theology stood still, nor because people gave up trying to make further theological definitions, but because the Crown resisted all attempts to produce a more elaborate or systematic form of doctrine. Thus we find that the Lambeth Articles (1595), which the strongly anti-Puritan Archbishop Whitgift drew up in order to clarify the Church's teaching on predestination, were never ratified by Queen Elizabeth I, and instead passed into oblivion. In 1615, the Church of Ireland produced articles that incorporated the Lambeth Articles and reflected ongoing theological developments in the Reformed world, and although they were accepted for a time in Ireland, they were eventually suppressed in 1635 at the behest of King Charles I. The *Westminster Confession of Faith*, composed in 1646, was largely the work of members of the Church of England and in that sense can claim to be an Anglican document, but it was rescinded in 1660 along with all Parliamentary legislation passed during the civil war and Commonwealth period (1640–1660). Since that time, there has been no attempt to produce an Anglican confession of faith, though various schools of thought have arisen within the Church and claimed to represent its theological inheritance. They may be classified as follows.

Puritanism

Puritanism was a movement for further reform of the Church of England after 1571. It reached its peak in the 1640s, but the Puritans were unable to agree on a common program that would unite the Church. The Westminster Assembly, which met from 1643 to 1653, produced a Confession of Faith, Book of Common Order, and two catechisms that were authorized by Parliament in 1646–1647 and remained "official" (in some sense) until the restoration of the monarchy in 1660, when they were rescinded. But even during the Commonwealth period, the decisions of the Westminster Assembly did not receive universal assent across the Church of England, where many radicals rejected all forms of church order and some conservatives secretly clung to the earlier pattern of Prayer Book worship. The Westminster standards were, however, adopted by the Church of Scotland in 1690, and they remain prominent in most Presbyterian churches to this day, a fact that tends to obscure their origin in the Church of England and the close theological relationship between Presbyterianism and Anglicanism.

Generally speaking, the Puritans accepted the Church of England's doctrine but rejected its unreformed pattern of discipline, which they sought to replace with their own, much stricter rules, and were unhappy with certain aspects of the Prayer Book, which they regarded as leftovers from the pre-Reformation Church of England. In 1662, about a thousand Puritan ministers left the Church of England to become "dissenters" or "non-conformists," taking their more devoted followers with them, but many did remain. Puritan theology survived, particularly at parish level, where interaction between conformists and dissenters was often frequent and productive. In some cases, dissenting ministers continued to attend their parish churches, and a few were even invited to preach from time to time. The idea that there was a great barrier between these two groups after the Restoration is a myth that has been demolished by the best modern scholarship. However, the belief that Anglicans and Puritans were opposing forces is still encountered in circles that have not kept pace with the latest research.

The first generation of Puritans included men like William Perkins (1558–1602), the most widely-read English theologian of his day. Later on, Puritanism was ably represented by Richard Baxter (1615–1691), who, although he left the Church of England in 1662, always sought a compromise and reunion with it.

ANTI-PURITANISM

Anti-Puritanism was a largely amorphous reaction to the Puritans that took different forms. Most anti-Puritans shared their Reformed theology but were content not to seek changes in church worship and government that the Crown would not support. They defended their position by arguing that the Puritans concentrated too much on secondary matters that were "indifferent" (the *adiaphora*). Most of the anti-Puritans were prepared to admit that, for example, episcopacy—the government of churches by bishops—was not essential to the life of the Church, and they recognized the legitimacy of non-episcopal Reformed churches outside England. But they also believed that each national church had the right to establish its own pattern of governance and to enforce it within its own jurisdiction. The Church of England was episcopal in structure, and so the anti-Puritans believed that everyone ought to accept bishops for the sake of order. It was precisely because episcopacy was theologically indifferent that it was not a matter for conscientious objection on the part of those who preferred something else, and so those of a conformist bent thought it should be accepted by everyone.

Leading anti-Puritans were John Whitgift (1530–1604), archbishop of Canterbury from 1583, who objected to Puritanism on disciplinary grounds, not theological ones, and Richard Hooker (1554–1600), whose position was similar. Later on, there appeared more theologically-motivated anti-Puritans like Lancelot Andrewes (1555–1626), John Overall (1559–1619), and, above all, William Laud (1573–1645), who, as archbishop of Canterbury from 1633, introduced measures that to some people amounted to persecution of the Puritan element in the Church.

It should also be said that there was in addition an influential group of theologians who were Reformed in their beliefs but generally stayed out of the Puritan controversy. Among them we may count John Davenant (1572–1641) and

James Ussher (1581–1656), the great archbishop of Armagh who was widely regarded as the most learned man of his time.

The post-civil-war settlement favored the anti-Puritans, particularly in the matter of episcopacy, which now became essential for the Church's government in a way that it had not been before. In particular, it became necessary for clergymen to receive episcopal ordination, though exceptions were still made for some who came from abroad, like French Huguenot pastors who were fleeing persecution at home. Many modern observers have dubbed those who actively supported this episcopalian establishment as "Anglicans" for want of a better term, but it would be more accurate to say that they were a faction within a wider Church that found itself on the defensive once the passions aroused by the conflicts of the Commonwealth period started to subside.

After 1662, the old divisions gradually gave way to new ones that may be classified as follows.

Low church

These were mostly people of broadly Puritan sympathies who remained within the state church after 1662. Low church people tried to find ways to accommodate the dissenters and generally welcomed them as much as they could. They did not break the law, but they stretched it, largely on the ground that if the matters of contention between conformists and non-conformists were truly *adiaphora*, they could be overlooked. John Edwards of Cambridge (1637–1716) was perhaps the most prominent representative of this school of thought.

HIGH CHURCH

These were the strict episcopalians who wanted to suppress all forms of Puritanism and at the same time distance the Church as much as possible from state control. They ran into trouble when King James II, a convert to Roman Catholicism, ascended the throne in 1685. This was because they accepted him as the supreme governor of the Church, even though he did not belong to it and (at least officially) regarded it as heretical. It was an impossible position for both the king and these high churchmen to hold, but when James was forced to flee the country and was succeeded by his daughter Mary II (1689–1694) and her Dutch husband, William III (1689–1702), many of them refused to swear allegiance to what they saw as an illegitimate regime. These "non-jurors" (as they were called) went into schism and, although few in number, had considerable support among the clergy, who regarded religious toleration as opening the door to unbelief and atheism.

It is this high church party that the inventors of Anglicanism in the nineteenth century regarded as the guardians of the true Anglican faith. They were dogmatic episcopalians, rejecting non-episcopal ordinations and churches that did not have bishops. They were staunchly orthodox in terms of the creedal theology they had inherited from the early church, but they were anti-Roman Catholic as well as anti-Puritan. They often stressed a kind of personal devotion that came close to salvation by works because of its emphasis on a methodical form of self-discipline that manifested itself in liturgical worship, fasting, and the like. The Wesleys were brought up in this tradition, and elements of what would later become Methodism were derived from it.

Among the high churchmen of this period, we may mention Jeremy Taylor (1613–1667) and, later on, William Law (1686–1761), who left the Church of England in 1714 because he refused to swear allegiance to the Hanoverian dynasty.

LATITUDINARIANISM

The latitudianarians were mainly clergy of an academic bent who rejected dogmatism in theology and promoted what amounted to freedom of thought. In liturgical matters they were usually closer to the low church than to the high, but they did not sympathize with Puritanism. For the most part they were supporters of what was coming to be known as the Enlightenment and were favored by the state, which wanted to remove religious controversy from the political sphere. High churchmen sought to excommunicate some of them for heresy and for a time were successful in doing so, but public opinion had turned against dogmatism in religion and after 1714 heresy trials became a thing of the past. The latitudinarians were the moderates of the eighteenth century, formally staying within the bounds of the established Church but frequently verging on unorthodoxy in their personal beliefs and tolerant of a variety of opinions that were undoubtedly heretical.

Latitudinarianism is hard to define, precisely because it was so broad, but among its more orthodox representatives we could mention John Pearson (1613–1686) and Edward Stillingfleet (1635–1699). With the rise of Enlightenment deism around 1700, these men became more conservative and, for much of the eighteenth century, represented "mainstream" Anglicanism in its defense against the new radicalism. Prominent among them were men like Edmund Gibson (1669–1748), Daniel Waterland (1683–1740), George

Berkeley (1685–1753), Joseph Butler (1692–1752), and William Paley (1743–1805).

Evangelicalism

Evangelicalism in the Church of England dates from the revival movement of the 1740s. It owed its origins to German Pietism, which tried to overcome confessional differences between Lutherans and Reformed Protestants by stressing a common devotional life and the necessity of a personal conversion experience. It was spread in England by John Wesley (1703–1791) and his brother Charles (1707–1788), and also by George Whitefield (1714–1770) and others. The movement soon split because the Wesleys were high churchmen and anti-Puritan in background, whereas Whitefield and most of the other revivalists were low churchmen with Puritan leanings. Eventually the Wesleyans left the Church of England and became Methodists, though the Wesleys themselves did not approve of secession from the established Church. The others generally remained within the Church of England, though there were some who became dissenters, particularly in places where the local Anglicans were hostile to the revival. The most influential Anglican evangelical was Charles Simeon (1759–1836), who in many respects was the shaper, if not the founder, of the movement within the Church of England. Today, evangelicalism remains strong, and in many parts of the world it is the dominant form of Anglicanism. It is also the branch of the Church that takes its historic doctrinal formularies most seriously and seeks to ensure that they remain its official teaching.

Evangelicalism was represented in the nineteenth century by men like John Charles Ryle (1816–1900), the only

Anglican theologian of his time whose works are still in print, and, more recently, by John Robert Walmsley Stott (1921–2011) and James Innell Packer (1926–2020). Also closely associated with the modern evangelical movement are Nicholas Thomas Wright (1948–) and Alister McGrath (1953–), both of whom reside in Oxford and continue to write extensively on theological topics.

ANGLO-CATHOLICISM

Anglo-Catholicism began as a reaction both to evangelicalism and to the moderate latitudinarianism of the eighteenth century. Its spiritual home was Oxford University, which is why it is often called the Oxford Movement. Its first proponents expressed their views in a series of *Tracts for the Times*, so the original Anglo-Catholics were called Tractarians. Basically, Anglo-Catholics rejected the Reformation, blamed the liberalism of modern society on Protestantism, and sought to revive what they thought was the Catholicism of the primitive church. To that end they rewrote the history of the Church of England, claiming that Anglicanism could be traced back to Roman times and that it was as independent of the papacy as were Eastern Orthodox churches. Over time they became more ritualistic in their religious practice and often copied Roman Catholic examples. The more extreme (or logical?) Anglo-Catholics tended to convert to Roman Catholicism as they realized that the Church of England was not truly "Catholic" in the way that they wanted it to be, but a significant number remained within the Anglican fold and sought to re-Catholicize it as much as they could.

Thanks to missionary work, there are parts of the world today where Anglo-Catholicism is the dominant form of

Anglicanism, but after a century of growth it is now in serious decline. Reforms in the Roman Catholic Church have thrown it off course to some extent, but developments within the Anglican world have also had their effect. Conservative Anglo-Catholics have been alienated by developments like the ordination of women, and the more liberal ones have often abandoned orthodox Christianity, keeping only the pseudo-medieval vestments and rituals that give a false appearance of traditionalism. Historians have also demolished their interpretation of church history, making it clear that what they claimed was a return to the sources of the faith was in fact a radical innovation without precedent in the Anglican world.

Leading Anglo-Catholics who did not leave the Church of England were Edward Bouverie Pusey (1800–1882) and John Keble (1792–1866). In the second generation were Charles Gore (1853–1932) and Robert Moberly (1845–1903), both of whom tried to engage with modern theological currents in ways that the original Tractarians would never have done. More recently the tradition has been continued by Eric Lionel Mascall (1905–1993) and popularized by Harry Blamires (1916–2017).

Liberalism

Also called *modernism*, liberalism in the Anglican Church claims to be an evangelistic movement in the sense that it is trying to "update" Christianity in order to make it more palatable to modern, secular society. The exact content of this liberalism is hard to pin down, and it keeps changing as the spirit of the age moves on to advocate new causes. It is relatively weak at grassroots level and almost non-existent in the developing world, but it is common in the higher echelons of the church hierarchy in both England

and North America. It is from this wing of the Church that the controversies of recent years over human sexuality have arisen. Liberalism has profited from the absence of effective church discipline and the growth of synodical government, because its advocates are often strongly represented in church administration, where they can promote change and even set the agenda for encouraging developments that are congenial to their outlook.

Prominent liberals of the modern period include Alexander Roper Vidler (1899–1991) and John Arthur Thomas Robinson (1919–1983), who popularized liberal ideas within the Church.

BROAD CHURCH

Alongside conservative Anglo-Catholics and evangelicals is a basically orthodox stream of Anglican opinion that has been more open to liberal ideas than either of the others but without succumbing to them. In many ways they represent "mainstream" Anglicanism in the modern world, though they have never formed a conscious "church party." Perhaps the earliest of these men was Frederick Denison Maurice (1805–1872), who is almost impossible to classify in traditional Anglican terms. More recently, the same could be said of William Temple (1881–1944), Clive Staples Lewis (1898–1963), Donald Mackenzie MacKinnon (1913–1994), Paul Avis (1947–), and Rowan Douglas Williams (1950–), each of whom has had significant influence on both Anglican and wider church affairs and theological discussions. In some respects, broad church people often appear to be more Anglican than either the evangelicals or the Anglo-Catholics because they are less likely to merge into non-Anglican bodies than are the other two. Also, they are often the dominant voice in intra-Anglican debates because they appear to represent a middle way between what are perceived as extremes.

THE ANGLICAN COMMUNION

The Anglican Communion is a grouping of forty independent churches (or "provinces," as they are usually called) that recognize the archbishop of Canterbury as their "head" and are in turn recognized by him. For the most part they are churches that have grown out of the Church of England, either by overseas settlement (as in Canada, Australia, and the United States) or by missionary work (as in most of Africa and Asia). A few churches, like the Church of Aotearoa New Zealand, combine elements of both, with Maori and Polynesian wings (*tikanga*) alongside the numerically dominant white settler church. The Anglican Communion also includes churches like the Lusitanian Church of Portugal, which broke away from the Roman Catholic Church in the nineteenth century and has now joined the Anglican Communion, even though it has no historic ties to the Church of England.

The Anglican Communion has no central authority and no power to discipline its members, as it has discovered to its cost in recent years. There have been various attempts to remedy this situation, but so far they have all failed because individual national churches do not want to surrender their autonomy. The Church of England probably could not do so even if it wanted to, because it is a state church beholden to the ultimate authority of the Crown in Parliament which would never be surrendered to an external body.

Anglican Churches are used to losing members to Rome or to more clearly defined Protestant bodies, and in recent years some have converted to Eastern Orthodoxy. But this movement out of the Church is counterbalanced by another one: growing numbers of Protestant evangelicals (in particular) being attracted to what they regard as Anglicanism. Usually they are drawn in by things like the liturgy and dignity of public worship, which is often lacking in their own churches, rather than by strictly theological matters. There is, however, a tendency for many of these people, who come from what Anglicans would describe as a very "low church" background, to go to the other extreme. In fact, not a few of them have used the Anglican Communion as a stepping stone on their way to Rome or the Eastern Orthodox church.

There are also some Roman Catholics who are distressed by scandals and the apparent immobility of the hierarchy in their own church who have left it to become Anglicans, though this seems to be the decision of isolated individuals rather than something that can be reasonably called a movement. In Latin America many nominal Roman Catholics have found a living faith in Anglican circles, where the charismatic movement has had a great impact. Whether (or to what extent) this will influence the course of worldwide Anglicanism remains to be seen. These people are often more concerned to define Anglicanism than others are, which puts pressure on the Church to articulate theological positions that most Anglicans have never thought about and (in some cases) that many have explicitly rejected. In the Anglican world, it seems that definition is almost bound to lead to exclusion, as one group or another finds itself outside the parameters laid down by those seeking a degree of theological clarity that has not traditionally existed.

Beyond the Anglican Communion

It must also be said that in recent times there have emerged a number of "Anglican" Churches that are not members of the Communion, usually because they have broken away from other Anglican Churches that are and so are not recognized by them. Some of these, like the Free Church of England, the Reformed Episcopal Church (in the United States), and the former Church of England in South Africa, now rebranded as REACH (Reformed Evangelical Anglican Church), go back to splits that occurred in the nineteenth century, but most of them have appeared recently, especially in North America, where they are usually conservative reactions to the liberal Episcopal Church and Anglican Church of Canada. Understandably, these groups are often much more self-consciously Anglican than their parent bodies are, but their relations with the Anglican Communion remain difficult. In some cases, they are recognized by Anglican churches or dioceses other than Canterbury, while the legitimacy of others is contested, particularly in the United States. For example, the Church of Rwanda, which is a recognized member of the Anglican Communion, has played an important part in the establishment of the Anglican Church of North America (ACNA), which is not. In England, some clergy and congregations have left the established church and joined the Free Church of England, apparently with the blessing of the local diocesan bishop who has promised to continue working with them in a different way. Whether (and how) anomalies of this kind can be resolved is one of the major questions currently affecting the Anglican world, and it is not clear how far the principles governing membership in the Anglican Communion can be modified in order to accommodate them.

At the present time, it is probably fair to say that Anglicanism is most acutely divided between liberals (strong in the first world) and conservatives, consisting primarily of evangelicals but also some Anglo-Catholics (especially in the developing world) and Anglicans who do not wear party labels but are concerned for the integrity of historic orthodoxy.

How this battle will play out is hard to say. Liberals try to establish themselves as the mainstream in modern Anglicanism, relegating their conservative opponents to a backwater where they will eventually atrophy and disappear. Conservatives, on the other hand, seek to reinforce traditional doctrine and have recently shown their strength in GAFCON (Global Anglican Futures Conference) and the overlapping Global South movement. It is possible that this conflict will only be resolved by a split that will create two Anglicanisms, something that already seems to be happening in the United States and elsewhere. It is too early to say how far this will go, but at the moment things appear to be moving in that direction.

COMMON CHARACTERISTICS OF ANGLICANISM

Anglican churches, whatever their origins, share certain characteristics that set them apart from other Christians, though to what extent they can be said to reflect a distinctive Anglican theology is not at all obvious and is debated within the Anglican world itself. These common characteristics can be listed as follows:

They all have an episcopal structure, which distinguishes them from many other Protestant bodies. Anglicans do not enter into formal union with other denominations unless they are prepared to take episcopacy into their systems, which they usually are, though there have been exceptions—the Church of Scotland, for example—and when that happens, full unity or intercommunion does not occur. Anglicans share episcopalianism with Roman Catholics and the Eastern Orthodox, though neither body recognizes Anglican bishops as canonically consecrated. As a result, Anglican episcopacy is in a curious position ecumenically, because on the one hand it is regarded as unnecessary by non-episcopal Protestants, and on the other hand it is seen as illegitimate by other episcopal churches that it claims to resemble.

They all have a set vernacular liturgy contained in a Prayer Book, though the content of this liturgy may vary considerably from one province to another. It is also true that recent liturgical revision and ecumenical convergence has made this characteristic less definitive than it used to be. Many churches, both Protestant and Catholic, now have shared forms of worship that make it easier for people to worship across denominational lines. At the same time, some Anglican churches, like the Church of Aotearoa New Zealand, have developed liturgies that are so distant from the classical model provided by the Church of England that it is hard to know whether they are really Anglican at all.

They all involve the laity in church government. Here Anglicans differ from Roman Catholics and the Eastern Orthodox, where the clergy dominate everything and lay people seldom have much of a voice. Clericalism is by no means absent from the Anglican world, but it is not intentional, and lay people are almost always represented in the synods and councils of the Church. In this respect, the decennial Lambeth Conferences that unite the bishops of the Anglican Communion are an anomaly, and the chances that they (or the even more restricted Primates' Meetings of the heads of the individual provinces) will ever acquire legislative authority are remote, despite occasional pleas for them to do so.

Anglicans have a hierarchy of beliefs that are rooted in their historic relationships to other churches and are set out sequentially in the Thirty-nine Articles of Religion. First come the catholic articles, which are intended to show that Anglicans confess the same basic faith as all other orthodox Christian churches. Secondly, there are the doctrines that make Anglicanism a branch of Reformed Protestantism. Finally, there are a few beliefs and practices that were designed specifically for the Church of England and may be irrelevant (or inapplicable) to other churches, including most Anglican ones.

These four characteristics are typical of Anglican churches worldwide, but only the last of them directly reflects Anglican theology. Anglican Churches are episcopally structured, but is episcopacy theologically essential to them? Some say that it is, and to them bishops are part of the being (*esse*) of the Church. Others say that it is not but agree that bishops contribute to the wellbeing (*bene esse*) of the Church, and so are prepared to accept them on that basis. These two viewpoints coincide with high and low church positions, respectively, and coexist in the Anglican Communion. The practice of episcopacy is universal, but the principles behind it are disputed, and so its place within Anglican theology is at best ambiguous.

The Prayer Book tradition reflects the Anglican desire to communicate theological principles through the medium of public worship, and ideally that is what a Prayer Book should do. Unfortunately, liturgical revision in recent times has seldom paid much attention to Anglican theology, and this failure has led to criticism and confusion in some cases. Modern liturgies are often worked out on an ecumenical basis and aim to reflect the earliest known forms of Christian worship, factors that tend to dilute their specifically Anglican character. That may not be a bad thing in some cases, but it means that Anglican liturgy is no longer a reliable guide to specifically Anglican theology and must be used with caution in determining what the latter is. The basic principle, established in 1850 by the Gorham Judgment on the nature of baptism, is that theology determines worship, not the other way around. Specifically, the Articles of Religion tell us what Anglican doctrine is and how the Prayer Book is to be interpreted. In the Gorham case, the widespread belief that Anglicans held to "baptismal regeneration" on the basis of words in the Prayer Book ("seeing therefore that this child is regenerate") was rejected on the ground that the Articles of Religion do not support such a view. Some clergymen left the Church in reaction to that, but the principle was upheld that "baptismal regeneration" is not an Anglican doctrine.

The role of the laity in the Church is important for the framing of Anglican doctrine, but it is not to be confused with that doctrine itself. The Anglican principle is that the Church's doctrine is a common confession of clergy and laity, both of whom share in its formulation. Historically this meant that the English Parliament had to approve the doctrinal standards established by the clergy (like the Thirty-nine Articles), and in England that is still the case, but nowadays all Anglican churches have synods in which lay people and clergy are both represented. These synods establish the

Church's doctrine, but it is not clear whether the synod of an individual member church of the Anglican Communion can legislate in a way that is opposed by other member churches (on same-sex marriage, for example) without forfeiting its membership in the Communion. Nor is it clear whether the Communion can establish doctrine(s) that all member churches must accept in order to remain in good standing. Here there is a significant area of uncertainty and disagreement with which the Anglican world must come to grips, and it is not yet clear what decisions will be taken or what effect they will have on Anglicanism as a whole.

ANGLICAN THEOLOGY

Where do we start when examining Anglican theology? Theology is basically the study of God, but to some people, everything to do with the Church is part of its "theology," whether it is directly connected to the doctrine of God or not. In the narrowest sense, there is no Anglican theology at all, because the Anglican understanding of God is essentially the same as that of virtually all other Christian churches. Many Anglicans would go further and say that Anglicanism has no features that are peculiar to itself. It is really what C. S. Lewis called "mere Christianity," or what John Stott called "basic Christianity." To have distinctive doctrines or practices would certainly set Anglicanism apart from other types of Christianity, but in the eyes of many Anglican apologists, it would be a denial of what Anglicanism stands for.

Yet whatever truth there is in this assessment, Anglicanism is not "generic" Christianity. It has a recognizable flavor of its own that has proved to be remarkably resistant to mergers with other types of Christianity, however much it may share with them. It has been remarked that Anglicanism is a "bridge church" with elements of both Protestantism and Catholicism, but the retort has sometimes been that if it is a bridge, it is one that does not touch either bank of the river. Somehow it sits in the middle without getting too close to either side. The differences between Anglicanism on the one hand, and both Protestantism and Catholicism on the other, are set in bold relief when the similarities are pointed out, making it more difficult to determine what Anglicanism actually is. The fact that some Anglicans lean more in one direction than the other complicates matters even more, since any attempt to define Anglicanism is bound to reflect the perspective of the speaker, which will almost inevitably betray a bias even when the presenter is trying to be fair to all sides.

It is perhaps best to say that the distinctiveness of Anglicanism does not lie in particular doctrines or practices that set it apart from other Christians, but in the manner in which those doctrines and practices are presented. To begin with, Anglicanism clearly belongs to the Western (Latin) branch of the pre-Reformation church. There have been times when Anglicans have developed close relationships with different Eastern Orthodox churches, and there are certain individuals who have pursued these connections at a deep level of engagement, but they are a minority, and their ecumenical outlook is unfamiliar to most member churches of the Anglican Communion. Relations with the Eastern churches have usually been friendly, but they are also rather distant, and reunion with them has never been a practical option. Anglicanism as we know it is one of the results of the great schism in the Western church that we call the Reformation of the sixteenth century. From that falling out have come the various Protestant churches and also the Roman Catholic Church, which went through a reformation of its own, despite its claim to be continuous with its medieval predecessor.

It is against the backdrop of the Reformation that the distinctiveness of Anglicanism must be measured. Which elements of the medieval church did it reject and which did it retain? Can Anglican bishops claim to stand in historic continuity with the bishops of the early church, even if the functions they perform are not the same? Or can it be argued that Anglican episcopacy is closer to that of the first Christians than are other modern forms of it, because in reforming medieval abuses the main aim was to recover the primitive pattern of episcopal oversight? Was that attempt successful, or are Anglicans fooling themselves in thinking that they have recovered a form of church government that in fact never existed? These questions, and others like them, have been answered by Anglicans in ways that set them apart from other Western Christians.

Today there is a spirit of ecumenism abroad that leads to friendly relations among churches that are not officially in communion with one another. This has led to a blurring of distinctiveness that many people think is a good thing, though others are afraid that it merely opens the door to confusion and misunderstanding. Is a distinctive Anglicanism worth asserting or defending in such a climate, and if so, to what purpose? Is Anglicanism better or worse than other kinds of Christianity, or just different from them? Are those differences a help or a hindrance to the church's primary mission, which is to preach the gospel and maintain the truth of the Christian faith in a world fundamentally opposed to the word of God? As always, Anglicans answer questions like these in different ways. Some actively work towards a goal in which Anglicanism will merge into a reunited Christendom and effectively disappear, whereas others think that what they see as its distinctive witness is needed now more than ever before. It is among this second group that Anglican theology is most likely to be expounded and promoted, though with very different outcomes, since those who value Anglican distinctiveness usually focus on some aspects of it to the neglect of others. In this process the fault lines of traditional Anglican divisions come to the fore once more, and defining what Anglicanism is becomes harder than ever.

Anyone approaching Anglican theology needs to bear these things in mind. No introduction can possibly do justice to everything that every individual Anglican believes, and the variety that can be found within the Anglican Communion will probably always be considerably greater than what the Church's official "formularies" (statements of belief and practice) prescribe. Nevertheless, the formularies are there, and even if they are often honored more in the breach than in the observance, they constitute a benchmark to which Anglicans eventually must return and against which they must measure up. New interpretations of them are always possible, but discarding them is not—at least not if the name "Anglican" is to be retained with any integrity.

The basis of any church's theology lies in its doctrine. Other churches have been quite clear about this. Most Protestant bodies have a confession of faith to which its ministers (at least) are expected to subscribe, and the Roman Catholic Church has a large body of official teaching that is expounded and monitored by the pope, whose interpretation is definitive for all Catholics, even if many of them reject it in practice. Anglicans, by contrast, have often been reluctant to define matters of faith too closely. Today, many would claim that Anglicanism does not have a confession of faith, and there is certainly no teaching authority equivalent to the papacy, but this claim needs some qualification. There is no Anglican confession that is theologically comprehensive and no document that defines the tradition in the way that the Westminster Confession does for Presbyterianism. But there is a statement of faith that was produced at the time of the Reformation and remains fundamental to Anglicanism as a distinct type of Christianity, because it expresses the Anglican position on the main points that caused the Church of England to maintain a stance independent of Rome and distinct from other Protestant churches. This is the text known as the Thirty-nine Articles of Religion.

The Thirty-nine Articles are seldom studied nowadays, but many Anglican churches, including the Church of England and the American Episcopal Church, print them as an appendix to the Prayer Book, and in wider Anglican circles they are still cited as a touchstone of Anglican orthodoxy. The nineteenth-century inventers of Anglicanism disliked them because of their Protestant origin and tried to minimize their importance, but in recent years they have reappeared, both in ecumenical discussions and in global Anglican contexts, and ignoring them in a definition of Anglicanism is no longer acceptable. As we have already seen, the Articles do not contain the sum total of Anglican theology, some of them now appear rather dated, and there are certain subjects that they (perhaps unfortunately) omit. But while they are neither comprehensive nor perfect, the Articles are the fundamental starting point for any serious discussion of Anglican theology. Properly analyzed and understood, they offer us a handy framework onto which additional material can be grafted in order to give us a reliable picture of what can legitimately claim to be Anglican. Individual Anglicans may disregard them or dissent from them to varying degrees, but the Anglican tradition as a whole continues to be shaped by them in both subtle and more obvious ways.

Perhaps the best way to understand how the Articles function is to think of Anglican theology in three parts—its *sources*, its *content* and its *application* to the life of the Church and its members. If we structure our presentation in that way, we shall be able to locate particular elements within the overall scheme and consider how they relate. Let us look at each of these three parts in turn.

SOURCES

The ultimate source of all Anglican theology is God. Without his self-revelation, there would be nothing to say, and Christianity itself would not exist. Who God is and what he is like must come first, since everything else flows from that. God has revealed himself in the Bible, the message that he has given through the prophets and apostles to the people of Israel and then to the Christian church. All Christians have received this revelation, but not all understand it in the same way. This is a good example of how Anglicans are at once one with the universal church and distinct, because, although we share the sources of our knowledge of God with all Christians, we interpret them in ways that set us apart from others at different points. The Articles therefore begin with the doctrine of God and expound it in a way that connects Anglicans with the wider church, before going on to expound their own distinctive approach to the subject.

CONTENT

Anglican theology has inherited a vast body of knowledge and understanding from the early church. In principle, it is open to considering any doctrine, idea, or practice that is part of the universal church's tradition, only reserving the right to evaluate it according to the degree that it conforms to the revelation contained in the Bible. If it is not found in the Bible, it cannot be imposed or adopted as a necessary part of Anglican theology, though that would not necessarily exclude it from consideration. For example, the veneration of icons that is practiced in the Eastern Orthodox churches is not found in the Bible, and Anglicans have not adopted it as part of their worship, but they do not condemn it or reject it outright. There is nothing in Anglican theology that says that an individual cannot use icons for spiritual edification, but because there is no biblical warrant for that practice, their use cannot be officially adopted or encouraged, let alone made compulsory.

On the other hand, there are some things that are clearly taught in the Bible and that Anglicans cannot ignore—like celebrating the Lord's Supper as central to regular public worship. The break with Rome in the sixteenth century was not just a schism; it was also a new departure in the way we do theology. The questions raised then were and still are fundamental to Anglican identity, even if they are not always in the forefront of discussion, and even though many people have never engaged with them personally. To be an Anglican is to belong to a tradition that has wrestled with certain issues and drawn particular conclusions from that struggle. Individuals today, and even whole churches, may have other priorities, but the founding principles of Anglicanism cannot be ignored. New ideas come along from time to time, but they fit into an existing framework and are inevitably shaped by that. The Articles set out what these founding principles are and explain how they have been received by Anglicans.

APPLICATION

Anglicans apply their theology through an episcopal structure of church government. They do so in a collegiate manner, involving clergy and laity as the bishops' equals. They do not conceal their faith in a foreign language like Latin, but instead speak in the language of ordinary people. Above all, they do not just talk about their theology; they turn it into a vehicle for worship. This is why the Prayer Book has such a central place in the Anglican world.

The *Book of Common Prayer*, as it is properly called, manifests a pattern of theology that Anglicans absorb every time they attend a service of worship. Inevitably, this will be the way in to the riches of Anglican theology for most people, but caution is required here. The Prayer Book is not a source of Anglican theology but a witness to its application. The principles on which it is built come from elsewhere, and its doctrine must be determined in light of the Thirty-nine Articles of Religion and the sources that they regard as authoritative (Scripture above all, and, in so far as they reflect its teaching, the three creeds, the *Homilies*, and the Ordinal).

The Articles themselves recognize other authorities, in particular the canonical books of Holy Scripture, and in that sense Anglican theology extends well beyond them and acknowledges sources that are more authoritative than they are. There is no conflict here. If Scripture (or the creeds) can be shown to teach something that contradicts an article, then it must be the article that gives way. But in practice, Anglican theologians usually maintain that the Articles are faithful to Scripture and the creeds and that they merely supplement them on matters that were deemed to be important at the time that the Church of England separated from Rome.

Since that time, various Anglican bodies have issued statements of a theological nature that have enjoyed varying degrees of acceptance in the wider Anglican world. In some cases, traditions like the monarchical episcopate have imposed themselves as the Anglican "norm," although they have never been formally defined as such. Does this make monarchical episcopacy a feature of Anglican theology or not? Some would say yes, on the grounds that faith and order belong together, but others would say no, claiming that Anglicans have been able to separate faith from order in a way that sets them apart from both Roman Catholics and many other Protestants. There is no definitive answer to this question that all Anglicans would accept, though many (if not most) would come down on one side or the other—and then insist that their view is the truly Anglican one.

In the past, episcopacy might have been regarded as a matter "indifferent," one of the *adiaphora* that the Reformers appealed to as a way of maintaining traditional practices without attaching particular doctrinal significance to them. In principle, this is probably still the official Anglican view, if such a thing can be said to exist, but individual Anglicans tend to reduce the category of what is "indifferent" by taking a particular position on the questions involved and then distancing themselves from those Anglicans who think otherwise. It is surely no accident that many of the controversies that have arisen within the Anglican fold have emerged in this way, as theologians and others have sought to define matters that were previously left undecided. The result tends to be that there are competing Anglican theologies, all of which can claim some basis in the Church's traditions, but none of which is in itself definitive of Anglicanism. The would-be neutral observer is therefore driven back to the concept of *adiaphora* as a device for reconciling two opposing views that have come into conflict at least partly because this concept has been ignored or devalued.

An introduction to Anglican theology has to take these tendencies into account, but it cannot be sidetracked by them into declaring as "Anglican" something like compulsory episcopacy that might be (and often is) legitimately disputed by other exponents of Anglicanism. The dangers here are clear for all to see. Leave these issues out and it will seem to many that vitally important aspects of Anglican theology have been ignored. Include them and there is a risk of being dismissed by those whose perception of the matters concerned is substantially different from the position preferred by the author of the introduction. There is no simple solution to this dilemma, and the reader must be warned that the *adiaphora* can be a minefield for the unwary. Diversity is undoubtedly a feature of modern Anglicanism, but comprehensiveness (in the sense of tolerance for opposing views) is rarer than that diversity might suggest.

To some extent, therefore, any introduction to Anglican theology has to include common foundations on which different edifices have been constructed by people who have believed (and often tried to persuade others to believe) the foundations were originally designed to support. In this sense, the Thirty-nine Articles of Religion remain the blueprint for the later work of Anglican divines. And it is by the

Articles that the theological stability of the structures added by later work must ultimately be judged.

It will be objected by some that the Thirty-nine Articles are a historical document of little relevance to the modern Anglican Church, and that they are largely unknown to most Anglicans today. This is true, but until 1975, incumbents of English parishes had to read them at their institution, and so congregations would have heard them from time to time, even if they did not know why they were being read. More importantly, ordinands (candidates for ordination) had to subscribe to them, and still do, if in a somewhat attenuated form. General ignorance of the Articles is therefore a failing of the modern Church, and it is not because they have been abolished or relegated to a secondary status. One of the encouraging signs of recent Anglican renewal is the increased attention that is now being paid to them again. Whether that will continue and where it might lead remain unknown, but it is too early to proclaim their demise, and now that more Anglicans are aware of the need to recover the common foundations of their identity, it may well be that they will regain some of the prominence that they have lost in recent times. What does seem certain is that no new confession of faith is likely to appear anytime soon, and so, with all their admitted limitations, the Thirty-nine Articles will remain the most important single source of distinctively Anglican doctrine for the foreseeable future.

PSEUDO-THEOLOGICAL CONTROVERSIES

A general discussion of Anglican theology would not be complete without some mention of what can only be called pseudo-theological controversies that have arisen in the past and that to some extent continue to characterize modern Anglicanism. At the time of the Reformation, relatively little attention was paid to the relationship between doctrinal principles and liturgical practices. For example, the medieval vestments worn by the clergy were retained, probably because they were not considered to be very important one way or the other. This indifference was questioned by John Hooper, who was nominated as bishop of Gloucester in 1550 but who argued that he (and the clergy generally) should dress differently if they were meant to be primarily preachers rather than celebrants at the Eucharist. Hooper refused to wear the traditional dress, and for that he was put in prison. This was not because of his views about the vestments but because of his disobedience to the rules still in force that governed such things.

Archbishop Thomas Cranmer believed that the continued use of vestments and other outward forms inherited by longstanding tradition should be kept so as to minimize the disturbance caused by liturgical changes, but Hooper and those who thought like him wanted consistency. To them, if a clergyman looked like a sacrificing priest, then he was a sacrificing priest—the vestments advertised a theology that the Reformers had rejected. They preferred the black academic gown that was worn in the universities as a more appropriate symbol of the teaching role that the clergy were meant to perform.

Another objection was put forward by John Knox, who thought that the practice of kneeling at Communion was a byproduct of belief in transubstantiation. He wanted to change the posture of the communicants, who should stand (or perhaps sit) to receive the consecrated elements rather than kneel in a display of what might be taken for adoration or veneration of the elements. Cranmer was prepared to accommodate Knox by inserting a rubric into the 1552 Prayer Book to say that kneeling did not imply adoration of any kind, though he did not go so far as to eliminate the practice itself.

The vestments controversy resurfaced in the 1560s, and Archbishop Matthew Parker was forced to issue a decree (or "admonition," as it was called) enforcing traditional practice but at the same time pointing out that, as with kneeling, the vestments had no theological significance of their own. As time went on, ecclesiastical dress became more simplified, to the point where, in the seventeenth century, the only thing still insisted upon was that the celebrant at the Eucharist should wear a white surplice and not a black gown. Even that was too much for many Puritans, who regularly disregarded the canon law that was supposed to enforce the rule and occasionally suffered punishment for their disobedience.

By 1662, most of the steam had gone out of the earlier arguments, and although Anglican worship remained more formal in appearance than was customary in nonconformist circles, the difference was not great enough to provoke much controversy. Over time, the question would probably have gone away entirely, but it was revived in the nineteenth century when a group of Anglo-Catholics turned to ritualism as an expression of their beliefs. They reintroduced medieval vestments and liturgical practices (like mixing water with the wine of Holy Communion) that had long since disappeared and were regarded by many as outlandish—and as signs of creeping Roman Catholicism.

Battles were fought over this, and some particularly zealous Anglo-Catholics were sent to prison for disobeying the law on such matters. Gradually their persistence paid off, and they were permitted to dress and act more or less as they pleased. Other Anglicans adopted some of their practices, like wearing a stole, but although things like that became so widespread as to be regarded as standard, they were never officially adopted, and no theological significance was ever attached to them.

The problem is that both the proponents and the opponents of vestments and the like believed that they did have theological significance, which is why they either promoted or rejected them. That significance was tied up with their view of the sacraments—the more elaborate the celebration, the more Roman Catholic the doctrine that lay behind it. Successive Anglican reports, synods, and pronouncements have repeatedly stated that neither vestments nor ritual gestures can have any effect on the sacraments themselves, so that what a celebrant does is ultimately a matter of personal preference and not a theological statement. That is the official view, and it allows people of very different opinions to work alongside one another, but it would be wrong to suggest that the controversies surrounding these things have been resolved. On the contrary, the high visibility of vestments (and, to a lesser extent, of liturgical acts) makes them immediate targets of theological disagreement, and for many people this constitutes the essence of the quarrel.

Visitors to an Anglican church today will soon detect whether it is "high," "low," or somewhere in between. Terms which originally referred to relations between church and state ("high" meaning less willing to submit to the state, "low" meaning more willing to accept a degree of state control over the Church), are now applied to liturgical practice, instead. Furthermore, they can arouse strong feelings, and in some places, those who favor one side or the other actively discriminate against their opponents. In England, for example, it is common for bishops to insist that ordination candidates wear a stole, even though it has no theological significance, and those who object (usually on theological grounds) can be given a hard time. Usually the bishop will argue that the stole must be worn for the sake of order and conformity, whereas those who object will say that if it is a matter of indifference, nobody should be forced to wear one. It is the old argument of order versus principle that inevitably takes on a theological coloring, even though it is not supposed to have one.

In purely objective terms, this is a pseudo-theological controversy, since theological arguments adduced (on both sides) are basically irrelevant. Unfortunately, this observation, while theoretically correct, does not cut much ice with those involved, with the result that vestments and liturgical practices become proxy excuses for waging theological warfare within the Anglican world—an unedifying spectacle that disfigures the Church but to which no satisfactory solution has yet been found. In recent years, some clergy have taken the radical step of returning to New Testament practice where (as far as we can tell) the celebrant(s) wore their ordinary clothes, but such is the legacy of controversy within Anglicanism that this very traditionalist solution is regarded as an extremely low-church phenomenon that may even be a provocation to those who are not like-minded. It is a reminder to us that, however hard we may try to keep them apart, theology and practice are not easily separated from one another, and that it is often the latter that is liable to influence our understanding of the former, which is the opposite of what ought to be the case.

▪ 2 ▪

The Catholicity of Anglicanism

(Articles 1–8)

Anglican churches all claim to be an integral part of the one, holy, catholic, and apostolic church that is confessed in the Nicene Creed. By far the greater part of their theology is shared with other Christians, and Anglicans have never claimed anything else. From the Reformation until today, almost everyone in the Anglican Communion has been concerned to stress this commonality, partly because they believe that it reinforces the integrity of Anglicanism as authentic biblical Christianity, and partly because it links Anglicans to all who confess the name of Christ. Anglicans have always claimed to be part of the one church but have never suggested that they are the only true church, or even the purest and best of the many denominations into which the universal church is now unfortunately divided.

The Anglican claim to catholicity does, however, have to be qualified to some extent in that:

1. Anglicanism belongs to the Western tradition of Christianity, not the Eastern one;

2. Anglicanism is Protestant, not Roman Catholic; and

3. Anglicanism is Reformed, not Lutheran, Anabaptist, or Pentecostal/Charismatic.

ANGLICANISM BELONGS TO WESTERN CHRISTIANITY

This is a distinction that is still relatively unfamiliar to many non-specialists, but one of the greatest and most enduring divisions within the Christian world is that between the Western (or "Latin") tradition and the Eastern (or "Greek") one. It is rooted in the cultural duality of the Roman Empire, where the Western half spoke Latin and the Eastern half Greek. The Eastern half was always more diverse, in that it included the non-Greek churches of Egypt, Syria, Armenia, and so on. It was also internally divided after the Council of Chalcedon in 451, when the Roman definition of the person of Christ as "one divine Person in two natures" was rejected by many in the East. These non-Chalcedonian churches still exist, but they are little known outside their home countries, and Anglicans did not have much to do with them before the great missionary expansion in the nineteenth century.

There was somewhat more contact with the Greek Church in the seventeenth century, but not enough to produce any lasting effect on either side. In modern times, emigration from Greece and Eastern Europe has created substantial communities of Eastern Orthodox Christians in English-speaking countries, but they tend to remain ethnically based—Russian, Romanian, Serbian, or Bulgarian as much as anything else. Their essentially mystical (or "apophatic") theology is little understood in Anglican circles, despite some effort to make it better known. For their part, Eastern Christians generally know very little about

Anglicanism and seldom engage with it at a serious theological level.

The Western tradition, represented above all by Rome but also by the Protestant churches that have broken away from it, is much more central to Anglican concerns. The Reformation was an exclusively Western affair, conducted in Latin according to theological concepts established by the medieval Western church. It is highly juridical in nature. A large part of our theological vocabulary reflects a background of law—justification, election, validity, etc. The way in which we express theological concepts and develop arguments (and counterarguments) comes straight from the medieval classroom, which was heavily influenced by legal antecedents. To put it succinctly, an Anglican in dialogue with a Roman Catholic may disagree with his partner on any number of issues, but he will be talking the same language. An Eastern theologian, by contrast, might wonder what the discussion is all about and fail to understand why it is important, because his mental framework of ideas is different.

ANGLICANISM IS PROTESTANT

There are some Anglicans who reject the term "Protestant" as a description of themselves, but they are a minority. Most are prepared to recognize that Anglicanism is an offshoot of the sixteenth-century Reformation, even if it has its own distinctive characteristics, and they are happy to describe themselves as Protestants. All Anglicans have to admit that they are not Roman Catholics, and since Rome brands all Western Christians who are not in communion with the pope as Protestants, they are forced to accept this designation whether they like it or not.

Anglicans are Protestants, not only because they reject the authority of the Roman pope but also because they have repudiated many of the practices and disciplines associated with the Roman Catholic Church. Anglican clergy are not obliged to be celibate. They have always worshiped in the living language of the people, not in Latin, as Rome did until the 1960s. They do not canonize new saints, and devotion to ancient and medieval ones, if not entirely non-existent, is not a major feature of Anglican worship. The Virgin Mary is not given the exalted status that she has in the Roman Church. Lay people play a significant part in Anglican church government, and Anglicans do not excommunicate people for disagreeing with pronouncements made by the church hierarchy. They also celebrate and receive holy Communion in both kinds—bread and wine, whereas Roman Catholics have habitually received the bread only.

Beneath these differences of practice lie numerous differences of doctrine, which formed the basis for the sixteenth-century Reformation. On matters like the supreme and unique authority of Holy Scripture, justification by faith alone, assurance of salvation, and the nature of the sacraments, the Thirty-nine Articles make it abundantly clear that Anglicans are on the side of Martin Luther and John Calvin, the great leaders of the Reformation in the German- and French-speaking worlds, respectively. Individual Anglicans may downplay or dispute their doctrines, but those who do are out of step with their Church. They may be strong and influential in some places, but in the Anglican Communion as a whole, they are a minority—and often an eccentric one at that. When controversies between Protestants and Catholics arise, as they have done over the ordination of women, for example, it is the (often liberal) Protestants who usually carry the day, leaving the dissenting (often conservative) Catholics to make their way to Rome.

This is not to say that all "Protestant" Anglicans support the ordination of women (many do not), nor that the "Catholics" who oppose it are wrong to do so, but only to observe that when arguments of this kind surface nowadays, it is more often the Catholics who are forced to give way and leave the Anglican fold because it is too Protestant (i.e., liberal) for them. Of course, that has by no means always been the case. In the nineteenth century, it was common for convinced Protestants to leave the Church because of what they saw as creeping Anglo-Catholic tendencies, and there are whole denominations, like the Reformed Episcopal Church in the United States, that reflect that trend. Today, conservative Protestants may still be inclined to leave the Church, not so much for that reason as because of the liberal stance many take on same-sex issues and similar moral questions, but this is a dispute among different kinds of Protestants. Those who leave Anglicanism for these reasons do not become Roman Catholics, and of course those who stay know that their Church's liberalism is pushing them further away from Rome than ever.

ANGLICANISM IS REFORMED

Within the Protestant world, Anglicans are more closely aligned to the Reformed tradition, represented by Presbyterians, for example, than to anything else. Once again, many individual Anglicans dissent from this analysis, pointing out (among other things) that the Reformed churches are usually non-episcopal, but these are differences of church government and not of theology. When it comes to the sacraments, for example, Anglican statements

on baptism and the Lord's Supper are much closer to classical Reformed teaching than they are to what is now
regarded as Lutheranism, something that many Lutherans
are quick to point out. Anglicans do not place the theology of Martin Luther at the center of their concerns in the
way that Lutherans do, and are generally more open to
Reformed influences, mediated through such figures as Karl
Barth (1886–1968), for example. It is true that in many parts
of the world, Anglicans have found it easy to work alongside Lutherans and to enter into communion with them, so
the differences must not be blown out of proportion, but
even so, classical Lutheranism appears strange to most of
them. Anglicans will sometimes debate the relative merits of
Calvinism and Arminianism (both forms of Reformed theology) but almost never discuss whether they are Philippists
or Gnesio-Lutherans in their approach to the Eucharist, not
least because (for the most part) they have no idea what
the historic controversy underlying that distinction was all
about.

It must also be borne in mind that the supreme governor
of the Church of England is a Presbyterian when she goes
to Scotland, not because she is expected to change her theological views, but because the two national Churches of the
United Kingdom are ordered differently. This flexibility is
possible because the Church of England shares a common
Reformed heritage with the Church of Scotland, allowing
the monarch to belong to both at the same time without sacrificing any significant theological principle. It is certainly
true that many individual Anglicans recoil at the mention of
Calvinism and do their utmost to distance themselves from
anything that might be associated with it, and it is also true
that Anglican worship is usually quite different from what is

found in Reformed churches in non-English speaking countries like the Netherlands and Switzerland. But the historical links with the Reformed tradition are still there, and the theological mentality is often close. Evangelical Anglicans, in particular, seldom hesitate to identify as Reformed, and many have taught at Reformed or Presbyterian seminaries without difficulty, something that would be harder to imagine with other Protestant traditions.

Anglicans have never had much sympathy with the radical Anabaptists of the sixteenth century, and the continued practice of infant baptism sets them apart from their modern heirs. Relations with Baptists nowadays are often friendly, but there is a clear difference of sacramental practice that prevents them from uniting, and even non-theologically minded laypeople are usually aware of that. The same must be said for Pentecostals and charismatics. Anglicans have been prominent in the charismatic renewal of the late twentieth century, and there are Anglican circles in which speaking in tongues and other spiritual gifts are present as a matter of course, but they are definitely in a minority. Anglicans may be less dogmatically opposed to these phenomena than some other Christians are, but they certainly do not promote them as an integral part of their Church's teaching, which generally says little or nothing on the subject.

On the other hand, it is this very silence on the matter, and the doctrinal flexibility that it permits, that has encouraged the growth of charismatic tendencies among some Anglicans, usually (though not exclusively) from an evangelical background. The well-known Alpha Course, based at Holy Trinity Church, Brompton (London), gives an Anglican stamp to a worldwide phenomenon that embraces all kinds of Protestants and many Roman Catholics as well.

This kind of Anglicanism may well be the most successfully ecumenical movement in the Christian world today, and is further evidence of how Anglicans, given the right circumstances, can reach across denominational boundaries that often seem to be impermeable, especially to those with more rigid doctrinal or ecclesiological commitments.

These necessary qualifications restrict the application of "catholicity" in the Anglican context, however sympathetic individual Anglicans may be to other currents of Christianity. In practice, there is much that Anglicans share in common with Christians of many different kinds. Within the above parameters, the first eight Articles of Religion state how Anglicans have received the catholic faith, and their tone indicates that the original compliers of the Articles believed that they were stating beliefs common to all Christians, even if that was not strictly true in certain details.

ARTICLE 1: OF FAITH IN THE HOLY TRINITY

> There is but one living and true God, everlasting, without body, parts, or passions; of infinite power, wisdom, and goodness; the Maker, and Preserver of all things both visible and invisible. And in unity of this Godhead there be three Persons, of one substance, power, and eternity: the Father, the Son, and the Holy Ghost.[1]

God is defined first, as he is in himself (without body, parts or passions), and second, as he appears to us (of infinite

---

1. All text of the Articles is taken from the original 1571 one. It is also the text reproduced in the 2019 ACNA Book of Common Prayer.

power, wisdom and goodness). His activity as Creator is then mentioned, as is the Trinity, defined as subsisting in the unity of the Godhead. None of this is new, and all Christian churches assent to the same teaching. Having said that, the approach taken here is typical of the Western tradition, and the wording reflects that of the first article of the Augsburg Confession, which Martin Luther and his colleagues presented to the Emperor Charles V at the Diet of Augsburg in 1530. Later Reformed statements of faith, beginning with the Second Helvetic Confession of 1566 and followed by such Anglican documents as the Irish Articles of 1615, put the doctrine of God in second place, after the doctrine of Scripture (the source of our knowledge of God), but this article reflects an earlier pattern that can be traced back to the creeds of the ancient church.

One apparent innovation in Article 1 states that God is "without body, parts, *or passions*." The doctrine of the impassibility of God was held by Christians from the earliest times, but it does not seem to have figured in a confession of faith before this. The addition was uncontroversial at the time, and it was later incorporated into the Westminster Confession. However, divine impassibility has come under scrutiny in recent years as theologians have wrestled with the need to express God's understanding of, and solidarity with, human suffering. The article implies that God's *nature* is impassable, but that does not preclude his personal involvement in human life. On the contrary, in the next article, the incarnation of the Son is explained by the fact that he had to acquire a human nature in order to be able to share in our suffering and death.

The distinction is an important one, because the suffering and death of the Son was not shared by the Father or the Holy Spirit. It was an act of the Son's divine Person, expressed in relationship to the human persons for whom he died. Our fellowship with God is personal, not natural or essential. We share in his eternal life without ceasing to be material creatures, and he remains what he always is—a divine being able to reach out to us in love without ceasing to be himself.

As understood in classical theology, divine impassibility was the assertion that God cannot be subjected to any outside power. If it were possible for another being to harm him, he would be inferior to that being, and that, in turn, would compromise his sovereignty over the created order. God is, and must be, immune to all that. Problems with the doctrine have arisen in modern times because the understanding of suffering has changed. We tend to think of it more in terms of sympathy (or empathy) with others, and thus conclude that if God is impassable, then he cannot relate to us in our suffering. This way of thinking is based on a misunderstanding. A person who is ill wants a doctor who understands his condition and appreciates how he feels about it. But at the same time, such a patient wants the doctor to cure him, not merely to share his pain, as the current saying goes. To do that, the doctor will probably have to be free of the pain himself, since otherwise he would be unable to operate effectively. Understanding the pain of others does not mean having to share it, as any mother who soothes her child's aches and pains will testify. Christians have always believed that God understands our suffering, that he has done something about it, and that he wants to apply the cure to us so that we can be set free from it. It is in that context that divine impassibility must be understood, and for that reason it is an important affirmation to make about God.

ARTICLE 2: OF THE WORD OR SON OF GOD, WHICH WAS MADE VERY MAN

> The Son, which is the Word of the Father, begotten from everlasting of the Father, the very and eternal God, and of one substance with the Father, took Man's nature in the womb of the blessed Virgin, of her substance: so that two whole and perfect Natures, that is to say, the Godhead and Manhood, were joined together in one Person, never to be divided, whereof is one Christ, very God, and very Man; who truly suffered, was crucified, dead, and buried, to reconcile his Father to us, and to be a sacrifice, not only for original guilt, but also for all actual sins of men.

The second Article is basically a restatement of the christological definition of the Council of Chalcedon, held in AD 451. That council divided the Eastern churches, which did not all agree that the incarnate Christ had two natures that were united in a single (divine) Person, but it was accepted by the West, and today both Protestant and Roman Catholic churches, as well as the Eastern Orthodox ones, confess it as a touchstone of orthodoxy. At the same time, modern Anglicans, like the other Chalcedonian churches, maintain friendly relations with the non-Chalcedonians (Monophysites and Nestorians) of the East, regarding the theological difference as more a matter of terminology than of substance. The word "nature" (*physis*) was not precisely defined at the time of the council, and the non-Chalcedonians took it to refer to the unity of the incarnate Christ. Chalcedonians do not dissent from that but use the term "nature" in a more restricted way, applying it to

Christ's humanity and to his divinity separately, but not in combination.

Also important is the comprehensiveness of Christ's sacrifice, made once for all in historical time and sufficient for both original and actual sin(s). This doctrine is elaborated further in the prayer of consecration used in Holy Communion (*Book of Common Prayer*). It undergirds the belief that human salvation can only come about by God's grace working though our faith and is not dependent on any works that we might try to contribute to it.

Original sin is the state of sinfulness that we have inherited from our first parents, whereas actual sins are those that we commit ourselves. Some people believe that it is unfair to count anything but actual sin(s), so that in their eyes, babies are born innocent. Anglicans, along with all other catholic Christians, reject this interpretation, saying that every human being is sinful from birth. However, this does not mean that human nature is sinful in itself, since, if it were, the Son of God could not have become a real man and remained sinless (see Article 15).

There was a latent tendency in medieval theology to say that Christ paid the price for original sin, which is taken away in baptism, but that we must do something to earn forgiveness for actual sin(s) because we have committed them as born-again Christians and therefore incurred responsibility for them. It was on the basis of that belief that the penitential system was erected, whereby individuals would do penance for the sins they have committed and seek forgiveness from God. By insisting that Christ died for actual sin(s), this article rejects any suggestion that something more than Christ's sacrifice is needed for our salvation. It also reassures us that every sin we commit—past, present and future—has been paid for by the sacrifice of Christ, so that we do not have to worry about falling out of a state of grace, as many medieval theologians taught. God's gift of grace is permanent and comprehensive, and those who are saved by it can rest assured that he will not desert them in their hour of need.

ARTICLE 3: OF THE GOING DOWN OF CHRIST INTO HELL

> As Christ died for us, and was buried, so also is it to be believed, that he went down into Hell.

Article 3 affirms that Christ went down to hell after he died, an obscure doctrine that is confessed in the Apostles' Creed but hard to find in the Bible. In its original form, this article was based the doctrine on 1 Peter 3:18, but the revisers of 1563 wisely abandoned that. No New Testament evidence for it is cited, but it is probable that greater weight was placed on Ephesians 4:8–10, as was the case in John Calvin's *Institutes*. The best explanation for this belief is that the suffering of Christ on the cross was more than just the propitiation for our sins. It was also victory over the power of the devil, who no longer rules the hearts of Christians. Believers do not have to worry that Satan might one day reclaim them and deprive them of the inheritance of eternal life in Christ. Nor is it possible for Christians to be demon-possessed. The power of Satan has been broken for good, and we have the assurance that we shall never again fall prey to his wiles.

Modern translations of the Apostles' Creed frequently remove the word "hell" and replace it with something vaguer, like "the dead," but this is not very helpful. For a start, who are these dead? Do they include those who have died in faith, awaiting the resurrection? If so, why would they need to have the gospel proclaimed to them when they have already heard and believed it? The term also excludes the satanic dimension, which defeats the whole purpose of the creedal assertion. Nobody likes to think about hell, but we are not supposed to be comfortable with it, and if we recoil from it, so much the better. The point of the article is that Christ has faced the worst and conquered it, for his glory and for our salvation.

ARTICLE 4: OF THE RESURRECTION OF CHRIST

> Christ did truly rise again from death, and took again his body, with flesh, bones, and all things apper-taining to the perfection of Man's nature; wherewith he ascended into Heaven, and there sitteth, until he return to judge all Men at the last day.

Article 4 affirms the bodily resurrection of Christ, a belief universally held by all Christians. Christ rose from the dead in the same body that suffered and died on the cross, though it had been partially transformed into a more purely spiritual nature. That transformation was completed by his ascension into heaven, where he remains in glory until his return to judge the world at the end of time. The important thing to remember about this is that the ascended and glorified Christ retains the wounds of his suffering on the cross, and that it is with these wounds that he pleads for us as our mediator in the presence of God the Father.

The article is intended to emphasize the physical reality of Christ's risen body, which is not a phantom or something different from our flesh and blood. At the same time, resurrection and ascension involved a process of transformation which will be replicated in us when we die and rise again to be with Christ. The difference is that what happened to him over forty days will happen to us in a single moment at the end of time. This is clearly expressed in 1 Corinthians 15:35–38, and the article must be interpreted in a way consistent with that. It should be noted that the phrase "perfection of man's nature" does not mean moral or spiritual perfection but physical completeness. There is no aspect of the human being that is not included in the resurrection, just as there is no part of us that has not been affected by the fall of Adam into sin.

ARTICLE 5: OF THE HOLY GHOST

> The Holy Ghost, proceeding from the Father and the Son, is of one substance, majesty, and glory, with the Father and the Son, very and eternal God.

Article 5 confesses the deity of the Holy Spirit, following the language of the Athanasian Creed, composed in southern Gaul (France) sometime around AD 500. It affirms the double procession of the Spirit from the Father and from the Son, a doctrine that is frequently known by its Latin abbreviation as *Filioque* ("and from the Son"). That was the teaching of Augustine, and it may even predate him in the Western church. The Eastern churches, both Chalcedonian and non-Chalcedonian, have never agreed to this, partly because they do not recognize the Athanasian Creed and were not consulted when the Nicene Creed was amended to include the *Filioque* (which some of them are prepared to accept as a permissible but not compulsory belief), and partly because many of them think that it is theologically wrong. Both of those positions are held within the Eastern churches, but Anglicans adhere to the traditional Western formula as it is confessed by all other Protestants and Roman Catholics. In response to modern efforts at ecumenical dialogue, it has been suggested that the use of the *Filioque* in the Nicene Creed might be made optional or discontinued, but attempts to give effect to that view have so far not succeeded, and in any case, dropping it from the creed would not affect the Church's confession as stated here.

The importance of the double procession of the Holy Spirit is that it explains how the Spirit is related to the Son, something that the Eastern churches regard as a mystery. It also guarantees that the mission of the Spirit will be balanced, giving equal weight to the other Persons of the Trinity and not favoring one over the other. Here the Eastern churches would agree with the West, because they posit a distinction between the mission of the Spirit (from both the Father and the Son) and the origin of the Spirit (from the Father alone). The Western churches do not make this distinction but argue that the Spirit's mission must reflect his origin if it is to be genuine. The issues at stake are hard for many people to grasp, but that does not mean that they are unimportant. The Western churches cannot simply drop the *Filioque* clause, because to do so would have unintended consequences for their theology, but neither do they wish to use it as a weapon against the Eastern churches. On the whole, it seems that most Anglicans, like other Westerners, are prepared to agree that there are different ways of looking at the Trinity, and that the Eastern formula has a validity within its own frame of reference. In this it must be said that they are more tolerant than are many Easterners—even today, the *Filioque* clause can raise hackles in the East to a degree that is unknown (and largely incomprehensible) to the West.

ARTICLE 6: OF THE SUFFICIENCY OF THE HOLY SCRIPTURES FOR SALVATION

Holy Scripture containeth all things necessary to salvation: so that whatsoever is not read therein, nor may be proved thereby, is not to be required of any man, that it should be believed as an article of the Faith, or be thought requisite or necessary to salvation. In the name of the Holy Scriptures we do understand those Canonical Books of the Old and New Testament, of whose authority was never any doubt in the Church.

Of the Names and Number of the Canonical Books

Genesis	The First Book
Exodus	of Kings
Leviticus	The Second Book
Numbers	of Kings
Deuteronomy	The First Book
Joshua	of Chronicles
Judges	The Second Book
Ruth	of Chronicles
The First Book	The First Book
of Samuel	of Esdras
The Second Book	The Second Book
of Samuel	of Esdras

The Book of Esther

The Book of Job

The Psalms

The Proverbs

Ecclesiastes or
Preacher

Cantica, or Songs
of Solomon

Four Prophets the
greater

Twelve Prophets
the less

And the other Books (as *Hierome* saith) the Church doth read for example of life and instruction of manners; but yet doth it not apply them to establish any doctrine; such are these following:

The Third Book
of Esdras

The Fourth Book
of Esdras

The Book of Tobias

The Book of Judith

The rest of the
Book of Esther

The Book
of Wisdom

Jesus the Son
of Sirach

Baruch the Prophet

The Song of the
Three Children

The Story
of Susanna

Of Bel and
the Dragon

The Prayer
of Manasses

The First Book
of Maccabees

The Second Book
of Maccabees

All the Books of the New Testament, as they are commonly received, we do receive, and account them Canonical.

All Christians accept the Holy Scriptures as the revealed word of God, and Anglicans are no exception. The emphasis of this article is on the sufficiency of the Scriptures for salvation. According to the article, things that Scripture does not contain (like the perpetual virginity of Mary, for example) are not essential to the faith and so cannot be required of any believer as necessary for his or her salvation. It follows from this that Christian doctrine must be based on the Bible. The article does not condemn nonbiblical beliefs or those who hold them, but rather regards such matters as speculative and therefore not part of the Church's official teaching. Here there is a clear difference between Anglican and Roman Catholic theology, because the latter insists on the acceptance of certain nonbiblical dogmas concerning Mary and the infallibility of the pope, which other Christians either reject or regard as private opinions rather than as compulsory doctrines. Anglicans are not forbidden to believe in the perpetual virginity of Mary, but as there is no evidence for that, they are not expected to teach it as something required for salvation—or even to suggest it at all. Christian doctrine must be grounded in what the Bible teaches and not be extended to cover pious opinions for which there is no basis in fact.

The article also outlines the canon of the Scriptures, making a difference between the Hebrew Bible and the Apocrypha, which appear only in the Greek translation popularly known as the Septuagint. The Septuagint was the Bible of the apostolic church, but the New Testament never quotes from the Apocrypha, leaving undetermined its status as canonical Scripture. The apocryphal books were not accepted as canonical by Jerome (d. 420), the great scholar who translated the Scriptures into Latin, but it was the contrary opinion of Augustine (354–430) that prevailed in the medieval church. In 1546, the (Roman Catholic) Council of Trent canonized the Augustinian list, and the

Protestant churches reacted by preferring the view of Jerome, as stated here. Nowadays there is general agreement among both Protestants and Catholics that the Apocrypha must be distinguished from the Hebrew Old Testament, and most would limit its use to what this article affirms.

One curiosity is that the list of Old Testament books does not mention Lamentations, though it was clearly part of the received Canon. The reason for that is that it was treated as an appendix to Jeremiah, though there is no evidence that the prophet actually wrote it. The names and order of the Old Testament books are a curious mixture of the Greek and the original Hebrew. For the most part, they follow the Greek pattern, but there are exceptions, like the books of Samuel and Kings, which are all called "Kingdoms" in Greek. Today, we follow the list as outlined here, except that "Ezra" and "Nehemiah" have replaced 1 and 2 Esdras in common usage.

Occasionally there are suggestions made that certain Biblical books are of secondary importance and/or should be dropped from the canon altogether. Even at the time this article was written, there were doubts about James (in the New Testament), but these doubts were ignored. Today it is possible, and indeed common, to use some books more than others, but it is highly unlikely that the canon will ever be formally altered. Within that limitation, Anglicans engage in biblical study on an ecumenical basis and are fully committed to using the best scientific tools for establishing the original texts and interpreting them correctly. Disagreements naturally continue to exist, but they are seldom if ever framed along denominational lines, and it is now virtually impossible to distinguish Anglican biblical scholarship from any other kind.

ARTICLE 7: OF THE OLD TESTAMENT

> The Old Testament is not contrary to the New:
> for both in the Old and New Testament everlast-
> ing life is offered to Mankind by Christ, who is the
> only Mediator between God and Man, being both
> God and Man. Wherefore they are not to be heard,
> which feign that the old Fathers did look only for
> transitory promises. Although the Law given from
> God by Moses, as touching Ceremonies and Rites,
> do not bind Christian men, nor the Civil precepts
> thereof ought of necessity to be received in any
> commonwealth; yet notwithstanding, no Christian
> man whatsoever is free from the obedience of the
> Commandments which are called Moral.

From its earliest days, the Church has accepted the Old
Testament as canonical Scripture, but knowing how to interpret it correctly has often been difficult. Anglicans are committed to reading it christologically. This article affirms the
unity of both Testaments in a single covenant, given by God
to Abraham and his descendants and fulfilled in Jesus Christ.
The ancient Israelites knew that their Scriptures pointed
toward the future coming of the Messiah, and pious Jews
waited expectantly for that to happen. They therefore interpreted the biblical text in that light, as did the first Christians.
At the same time, the coming of Christ has transformed the
framework (or "dispensation") in which the eternal covenant
is administered. Unlike ancient Israel, the Christian church
does not constitute a visible nation, and Christians have no
need to perform rites and ceremonies that were designed to
herald the Messiah's coming and have been made redundant

by his sacrifice and death. But the moral demands of the Mosaic law have not been annulled. On the contrary, as Jesus taught, they have been internalized and made even stricter than they were before. The prohibitions of murder and adultery, for example, have now been extended to include evil thoughts as well as actual deeds, making the ancient commandments of more universal application than they might have seemed before.

The article appears to distinguish three types of law in the Old Testament—ceremonial, civil, and moral, a categorization that modern scholars generally reject. But a careful reading of the article shows that it does not necessarily support a crude division of that kind. It talks about *aspects* of the one law of Moses, not about *categories* into which that law can be analyzed. It is therefore possible to accept the modern understanding of the law without denying or abandoning the way in which it is presented in this article.

ARTICLE 8: OF THE THREE CREEDS

> The Three Creeds, *Nicene* Creed, *Athanasius's* Creed, and that which is commonly called the *Apostles'* Creed, ought throughly to be received and believed: for they may be proved by most certain warrants of Holy Scripture.

This article affirms that the three creeds inherited from the ancient church are orthodox because what they say conforms to the teaching of the Scriptures. Their authority for establishing the church's doctrine is secondary and derivative, but they are important because they distill the message of the entire Bible in a few short lines. The creeds were memorized by both clergy and laity and served as a guide to the message of the Bible. In the sixteenth century, it was generally believed that the Nicene Creed had been composed at the first Council of Nicaea in AD 325, and that the Athanasian Creed was the work of St. Athanasius (296–373), whose one-man stand for orthodoxy in the face of Arianism had passed into legend. For much of the middle ages, it had been thought that the Apostles' Creed was the work of the apostles themselves, but by the time this article was composed, doubts had arisen on that score, and they are reflected in the way the Article is phrased.

Today we know that none of the creeds were written by those to whom they are attributed. Primitive forms of the Apostles' Creed can be traced back to the late second century, but the form in which we now know it dates only from the writings of Pirminius of Reichenau in the early 700s. The Nicene Creed may have been composed at or shortly after the first Council of Constantinople in 381, but the first mention of the text as we now have it is connected to the Council of Chalcedon (AD 451). As for the Athanasian Creed, it was written in Latin sometime around AD 500, more than a century after the great bishop's death, and is unknown in the Eastern church. The names attributed to the creeds represent the doctrine that the apostles, the first Council of Nicaea, and Athanasius were believed to have taught, not what they themselves wrote. Understood in this way, the Creeds represent the consensus of the ancient Western church, and there is nothing surprising or unusual about their acceptance by Anglicans.

Today, the Apostles' and the Nicene Creeds are in regular use in most Anglican churches, but the Athanasian Creed is seldom heard. It is included in the 1662 *Book of*

Common Prayer and authorized as a replacement for the
Nicene Creed on thirteen days in the year, but the American
Episcopal Church dropped it entirely in 1801, almost certainly because of its damnatory clauses at the beginning and
the end. These state that anyone who does not believe the
creed will "perish everlastingly," a sentiment disliked in the
age of Enlightenment. However, the creed's purpose is to
insist that the Christian faith demands intellectual commitment to the truth of revelation, with dire consequences for
those who openly reject it. The creed is important mainly
for its careful exposition of the unity and Trinity of God,
as confessed in Article 1, and it should be retained for that
purpose at least.

▪ 3 ▪

The Reformed (Protestant) Character of Anglicanism

(Articles 9–33)

T he main body of the Thirty-nine Articles is devoted to an explanation of the Reformed faith as accepted by the Anglican tradition. Many aspects of it are shared with other Christians, and these articles (9–33) should not be read as if they were deliberately trying to exclude them. Rather, they are outlining the way of salvation as revealed in Holy Scripture and confessed by Reformed churches. Anglicans do not deny that other formulations of the same faith are possible, but accept that this is the way that their own tradition has received it, and that it was the great controversies of the sixteenth-century Reformation that compelled the Church of England to take the stand that it did. Most Protestant denominations have statements of faith that are broadly compatible with these articles, though as with the Catholic ones, there are points of detail on which some differ. Many would also go further than these articles do in developing certain aspects of particular doctrines, notably predestination and the doctrine of the church. Anglicans are free to follow them in this if they want to, but they are not compelled to go beyond what the articles affirm. Where there is evidence of controversy among Protestants (as in Article 29, for example), Anglicans have typically come down on the Reformed side, as opposed to the Lutheran. In the past, that prevented closer links with the Lutherans, but in modern times those differences have either been resolved by discussion or sidelined as secondary matters that should not impede mutual recognition and fellowship.

The Reformed Articles can be subdivided and analyzed as follows, with the second section further subdivided:

- Articles 9–18: The Way of Salvation (also called the *ordo salutis* in Latin)

- Articles 19–33: Church, Ministry, and Sacraments

- Articles 19–22: Church

- Articles 23–24: Ministry

- Articles 25–33: Sacraments

These divisions are not hard and fast, because the ministry and the sacraments overlap, but insofar as a pattern can be discerned, this seems to be the most accurate and serviceable one. It will become apparent that the way of salvation, although it is expressed in Protestant terms and in the context of sixteenth-century controversies, is meant to be common to all Christians, and is in fact shared by Protestants across the board. There is no difference here between Lutherans and Reformed, and the Articles in this section are mostly drawn from, and expressed in accordance with, the teaching of Martin Luther himself, most notably in his treatise *On the Bondage of the Will* and in his two series of *Lectures on Galatians*.

THE WAY OF SALVATION
(*ORDO SALUTIS*)

ARTICLE 9: OF ORIGINAL OR BIRTH-SIN

> Original Sin standeth not in the following of *Adam*,
> (as the *Pelagians* do vainly talk;) but it is the fault and
> corruption of the Nature of every man, that naturally
> is ingendered of the offspring of *Adam*; whereby man
> is very far gone from original righteousness, and is of
> his own nature inclined to evil, so that the flesh lusteth
> always contrary to the Spirit; and therefore in every
> person born into this world, it deserveth God's wrath
> and damnation. And this infection of nature doth
> remain, yea in them that are regenerated; whereby the
> lust of the flesh, called in the Greek, φρόνημα σαρκός,
> which some do expound the wisdom, some sensuality,
> some the affection, some the desire, of the flesh, is not
> subject to the Law of God. And although there is no
> condemnation for them that believe and are baptized,
> yet the Apostle doth confess, that concupiscence and
> lust hath of itself the nature of sin.

This article sets out the human condition that has made
salvation necessary. In its broad outlines, it is shared by all
Christians, but there are certain emphases that have been
obscured or misinterpreted at different times. Pelagius, an
early fifth-century British monk, apparently taught that
everyone is born sinless, becoming guilty only when they
reach the age at which they consciously sin. This has never
been orthodox Christian teaching, but in the sixteenth century there were many who thought that it was the doctrine

of the Anabaptists. Their rejection of infant baptism was mistakenly believed to indicate a denial of original sin.

The main thrust of the article is that original sin is not removed by baptism, as many medieval theologians had taught. On the contrary, it remains in the human being throughout his or her earthly life. Christians are not condemned because of it, but they must accept its continuing existence and that its power is still at work in their lives. Salvation is not a once-off deliverance from sin, but the giving of spiritual grace sufficient to deal with it and to overcome it.

It is interesting to note that the article recognizes that a single Greek phrase can be translated in many different ways, even when the general idea is clear enough. The important thing is that human beings are naturally hostile to God and disobedient to his will—precisely how this is described is a secondary matter. In many ways this is typical of Anglican theology, which allows for a variety of expression as long as the fundamental concept is understood. The phrase itself is found in Romans 8:6, one of the key New Testament passages dealing with the nature of salvation and the Christian life. The King James version of 1611 translates it as "the carnally minded," making it refer to people rather than to an idea, and contrasts it with "spiritually minded," literally "mind of the Spirit" (*phronema tou pneumatos*). The meaning is clear enough, and it recurs at regular intervals in the Pauline Epistles, often with slightly different terminology. Thus in 1 Corinthians 2:14, Paul talks about the *psychikos anthropos*, contrasting him with the *pneumatikos anthropos* ("spiritual man"). There is no problem understanding what he means by *psychikos anthropos*, but finding an adequate translation in English is almost impossible, because there is no equivalent of *psychikos* in our language. Like the authors of this article, we are forced to find an equivalent expression (like "unspiritual man"), which is not an exact translation but does duty for "psychic," "animal," and "soulish," none of which is really possible in this context.

ARTICLE 10: OF FREE-WILL

> The condition of Man after the fall of *Adam* is such, that he cannot turn and prepare himself, by his own natural strength and good works, to faith, and calling upon God: Wherefore we have no power to do good works pleasant and acceptable to God, without the grace of God by Christ preventing us, that we may have a good will, and working with us, when we have that good will.

This article states that free will, in the sense that Adam and Eve possessed it, no longer exists. Every human being is born a sinner, and there is no way that we can escape from that condition by our own efforts. Even if we do good things, they do not earn merit with God unless and until the grace of Christ is present in our lives. Good works, in other words, are the consequence of salvation and cannot help to cause it.

Human beings have fallen into spiritual slavery as a result of sin. Some people interpret a denial of human free will as meaning that we are robots or puppets in the hand of God, but that is not true, and is not what is being stated here. We are like fish in an aquarium—free to move around, but limited by a framework that we cannot escape. Nobody can choose not to be a sinner, so that whatever we do, even if it is something that we decide for ourselves, shares the character of sin and is unable to deliver us from it.

The fundamental idea being asserted here is the same as that found in Martin Luther's famous treatise *On the Bondage of the Will*, which he wrote in response to Erasmus, who claimed that human beings are free to choose between right and wrong. Erasmus enjoyed a high reputation in England because of his scholarship, so it is especially significant that on this key point, the Church of England came down very much on the side of Luther.

ARTICLE 11: OF THE JUSTIFICATION OF MAN

> We are accounted righteous before God, only for the
> merit of our Lord and Saviour Jesus Christ by Faith,
> and not for our own works or deservings: Wherefore,
> that we are justified by Faith only is a most whole-
> some Doctrine, and very full of comfort, as more
> largely is expressed in the Homily of Justification.

The doctrine of justification by faith alone was the central teaching of the Lutheran Reformation and is fully accepted by Anglicans. Apart from anything else, it is a guarantee that everyone is saved equally—there is no special reward for those who do more (or better) works than others. Likewise, none of us can boast of our achievements before God or ask for special treatment in view of the efforts we have made. All credit (merit) belongs to Jesus Christ the Savior, and it is only by faith in him and in the efficacy of his sacrifice that we can be considered "righteous" and stand blameless in the presence of God.

The article does not spell out the doctrine of justification in detail, but refers us to the "Homily of Justification." This is the third sermon in the *First Book of Homilies* (1547), where it is called the "Homily of Salvation." It is a reminder to us of the importance of the *Homilies* as a source of Anglican doctrine. The Articles are meant to be read in the light of them, and in particular of the six doctrinal ones contained in the *First Book*. The *Homilies* were intended to be read in churches, particularly by those ministers who did not have a license to preach, and were a means by which Reformed doctrine was conveyed to lay people, as well as to the clergy.

The essence of this article is that there is no such thing as human righteousness. Nothing that we think, say, or do is able to overcome the barrier of sinfulness that separates us from God. The only way that we can have fellowship with him is by being united to him in the trusting relationship of faith. We dedicate our lives to him, and he asks the Father to forgive us on the grounds that he has extended his righteousness to cover us as well, even though we are unworthy to receive it.

In one sense, this is a very simple doctrine, but it goes against the grain for many people, who want to believe that they can contribute to their salvation or even earn it. Such people may mean well, but, as Anselm of Canterbury remarked to his pupil Boso, they have underestimated the seriousness of sin and the necessity of God's saving grace. Sin is too pervasive for us to be able to limit its effects, but God's grace is sufficient to meet our every need, so that our own feeble efforts are not only inadequate but redundant.

Article 12: Of Good Works

> Albeit that Good Works, which are the fruits of Faith,
> and follow after Justification, cannot put away our
> sins, and endure the severity of God's Judgement; yet
> are they pleasing and acceptable to God in Christ,
> and do spring out necessarily of a true and lively
> Faith; insomuch that by them a lively Faith may be as
> evidently known as a tree discerned by the fruit.

This article explains the proper place of good works in the
Christian life. They are useless for earning our salvation,
which is a gift of grace in and through Jesus Christ, but
they are the necessary consequence of it, and in that sense
they are pleasing to God. Christians cannot simply claim
to believe the gospel; they must demonstrate their commitment to that belief by the way they live.

Good works cannot earn salvation because they are
inadequate to meet the need. The other problem is that if
our good works were to be counted, some people would
be in a better situation than others because they would
have been more successful at doing good works. There is
no hierarchy of that kind in heaven, where everyone gets
the same reward.

At the same time, because we are grafted into Christ like
branches of a tree. no Christian is dispensed from doing as
much good as possible. The fruit we bear reflects the quality
of the connection we have with that trunk. If there is no fruit
to be seen, we must question whether the branch is really
grafted into the tree—and probably conclude that it is not.

This article is an important corrective to the idea, put forward by Catholic opponents of the Reformation, that a doctrine of justification by faith alone leads inevitably to an indifference to sin among Christians. Those who are justified by faith are meant to demonstrate that fact by the way they behave, a doctrine that is common to all Protestants, including Anglicans.

ARTICLE 13: OF WORKS BEFORE JUSTIFICATION

> Works done before the grace of Christ, and the Inspiration of his Spirit, are not pleasant to God, forasmuch as they spring not of faith in Jesus Christ, neither do they make men meet to receive grace, or (as the School-authors say) deserve grace of congruity: yea rather, for that they are not done as God hath willed and commanded them to be done, we doubt not but they have the nature of sin.

Anglicans reject that human beings can earn rewards from God by their good works. No person can contribute to his or her own salvation, however much he or she might want to. Nobody is entitled to salvation on the basis of personal achievement, and those who think (or hope) they are make things worse by committing a sin in the eyes of God.

The School authors—the scholastic theologians of the twelfth century and later—developed a systematic theology that was taught in the medieval schools, or universities. The tradition originated in Paris with Peter Lombard (1090–1160) and was carried on by great men like Thomas Aquinas (1226–1274) and others. They were accused of analyzing the way of salvation to the point that it disappeared altogether. That was unfair in some ways, but the practical consequences of their teaching had led the medieval church away from a clear proclamation of the gospel.

Anglicans have always rejected scholasticism in favor of a theology based on the doctrine of justification by faith alone. The concept of "congruity" states that while human efforts can never measure up to the demands of God, they can nevertheless match them in some way. The idea is that if we do our best with the right intentions, God will honor that, even if our actual achievements fall short of his requirements. This article teaches that apart from faith in Jesus Christ, no human action has any saving merit attached to it, for the simple reason that human beings cannot save themselves by their own efforts. Those who are locked in sinfulness cannot escape it, and so whatever they do will be tainted by sin.

Article 14: Of Works of Supererogation

> Voluntary Works besides, over, and above, God's Commandments, which they call Works of Supererogation, cannot be taught without arrogancy and impiety: for by them men do declare, that they do not only render unto God as much as they are bound to do, but that they do more for his sake, than of bounden duty is required: whereas Christ saith plainly, When ye have done all that are commanded to you, say, We are unprofitable servants.

Medieval theologians taught that there was some merit in doing more than is required by the law. It is the principle of "going the extra mile," something that may be good in itself but has no value for our salvation. The problem was that the church had been teaching that this superfluous merit could be stored up and used to mitigate unconfessed sins, or sins for which adequate penance had not been done. Anglicans repudiate the idea that sins can be calculated and traded off in this way.

The truth is that since no human works have any saving merit in the eyes of God, going beyond what is required by the law is irrelevant. No matter how much we do, we still fall far short of what God demands, and to imagine otherwise is a delusion. Unfortunately, it is a trap that many people fall into, and it can become a source of pride, which is the chief of sins. In this way, what appears on the surface to be good can become a source of grief to those who place their trust in such behavior. Christians must not be led astray by false hopes and promises, and must instead remember that even when we have done our best, in the eyes of God we remain "unprofitable servants." This was what Jesus taught his disciples (Luke 17:10), and the same principle applies to us as well.

Article 15: Of Christ alone without Sin

> Christ in the truth of our nature was made like unto us in all things, sin only except, from which he was clearly void, both in his flesh, and in his spirit. He came to be the Lamb without spot, who, by sacrifice of himself once made, should take away the sins of the world, and sin, as Saint *John* saith, was not in him. But all we the rest, although baptized, and born again in Christ, yet offend in many things; and if we say we have no sin, we deceive ourselves, and the truth is not in us.

Jesus Christ, though fully human, was also sinless, which makes him unique. What this Article teaches is that sin does not reside in our physical natures but in our spiritual persons, which have rebelled against God. Jesus was the divine Person of the Son who took on a human nature. He was without sin because of his divine personhood and was therefore able to take our sins upon himself and pay the price for them. No other human being, however holy he or she may be, can come anywhere near to this, because sinfulness remains present in us, even if we have been baptized and are living the kind of life that Jesus has prescribed for us. We are protected from sin by grace, whereas he was free of it by nature.

Much of this article is a quotation from 1 John 1:8–10 and other verses later in the same epistle. Jesus Christ is the Son of God because he is God and cannot sin. We can become "sons of God" by adoption, but our entitlement to that status rests on our union with the natural Son, and not on anything that we are or have in ourselves. If that union is broken or compromised, our participation in Christ's righteousness suffers accordingly, because sin is always present and active in us, whether we like it or not.

A Christian who imagines that by being united with Christ in baptism and regeneration he or she is thereby set free from sin is deluded. Christians are not little imitations of Christ, because if they were, they would not need him as their Savior. The truth is believers are always fully dependent on Christ, who has taken away our sin by his sacrifice on the cross.

It can also be said on the basis of this article that there is no sin so great Christ cannot forgive it. Some people imagine that they have sinned too much to be able to be forgiven, but the gospel message says this is not the case. All who repent and believe have their sins pardoned, however great and seemingly intractable those sins may have been. The saving grace of God is greater than anything human beings can do to reject it, and Christ's sacrifice is sufficient to save even the worst of sinners.

Article 16: Of Sin after Baptism

> Not every deadly sin willingly committed after Baptism is sin against the Holy Ghost, and unpardonable. Wherefore the grant of repentance is not to be denied to such as fall into sin after Baptism. After we have received the Holy Ghost, we may depart from grace given, and fall into sin, and by the grace of God we may arise again, and amend our lives. And therefore they are to be condemned, which say, they can no more sin as long as they live here, or deny the place of forgiveness to such as truly repent.

It was believed by many Christians in the early church period that sins were taken away in baptism, and that if a baptized person sinned again, he or she would lose his or her salvation, because there was no further remedy for the offense committed. That teaching had persuaded some people to defer their baptism until just before their death, so as not to run such a risk. It was an obvious travesty of the gospel, since to reserve baptism for the last moments on earth was effectively to deny the possibility of living a Christian life in this world, which believers are obviously called to do. The solution to this apparent problem was provided by Augustine of Hippo (354–430), and this article reflects his teaching on the subject, which the Reformers also accepted.

All Christians continue to sin after baptism, because sinfulness is inherent in us. It is possible for believers to commit even very serious sins without losing their salvation, because there is always the possibility of repentance and restoration. The gospel offers us a fresh start, even if we are already believers.

The Holy Spirit dwells in our hearts by faith, but he does not automatically prevent us from sinning, nor do our sins necessarily constitute blasphemy against him. This matters because Jesus taught that blasphemy against the Holy Spirit would not be forgiven (Matt 12:31), but that teaching does not apply to believers who repent of their sins and amend their lives accordingly. The article does not explain what the blasphemy against the Holy Spirit is, but we may safely assume that those who are guilty of it will not be led to repentance and therefore they will not receive the forgiveness they need to restore them to life in Christ.

The article also reminds us that those who claim that it is possible to attain sinless perfection in this life are fooling themselves, and their pretensions must be rejected. Likewise, those who truly repent will be forgiven, and to say that they will not be is to deny the grace of Christ. The church is a body of repentant sinners, none of whom is rejected but none of whom has advanced so far along the path of righteousness that he or she has no more need for Christ's grace.

ARTICLE 17: OF PREDESTINATION AND ELECTION

Predestination to Life is the everlasting purpose of God, whereby (before the foundations of the world were laid) he hath constantly decreed by his counsel secret to us, to deliver from curse and damnation those whom he hath chosen in Christ out of mankind, and to bring them by Christ to everlasting salvation, as vessels made to honour. Wherefore, they which be endued with so excellent a benefit of God be called according to God's purpose by his Spirit working in due season: they through Grace obey the calling: they be justified freely: they be made sons of God by adoption: they be made like the image of his only-begotten Son Jesus Christ: they walk religiously in good works, and at length, by God's mercy, they attain to everlasting felicity.

As the godly consideration of Predestination, and our Election in Christ, is full of sweet, pleasant, and unspeakable comfort to godly persons, and such as feel in themselves the working of the Spirit of Christ, mortifying the works of the flesh, and their earthly members, and drawing up their mind to high and heavenly things, as well because it doth greatly estab-lish and confirm their faith of eternal Salvation to be enjoyed through Christ, as because it doth fer-vently kindle their love towards God: So, for curi-ous and carnal persons, lacking the Spirit of Christ, to have continually before their eyes the sentence of God's Predestination, is a most dangerous down-fall, whereby the devil doth thrust them either into desperation, or into wretchlessness of most unclean living, no less perilous than desperation.

Furthermore, we must receive God's promises in such wise, as they be generally set forth to us in Holy Scripture; and, in our doings, that Will of God is to

> be followed, which we have expressly declared unto
> us in the Word of God.

This, the longest of the Articles, deals with the sensitive subject of predestination. Anglicans are fully committed to what some have called the "Augustinian" doctrine of predestination, which is clearly taught in the New Testament and has always been officially accepted by both Protestant and Roman Catholic churches. However, many people within those churches have resisted what they see as its unfairness. In their view, people ought to be given a choice as to whether to follow God or not. The idea that this has somehow been determined in advance is obnoxious to them because it appears to reduce human beings to the status of robots.

To counter this, Anglicans teach that God made the world for a purpose, part of which was to redeem his chosen ones and grant them everlasting salvation. These people, called the "elect," have been set apart by God from all eternity, but their calling only becomes visible in the course of their lives on earth. As we see it from our limited vantage point in time and space, such people are progressively called by the Holy Spirit and respond to his voice. They are then justified by grace through faith, adopted as children of God, and transformed into men and women who do his will. They have the assurance that when they die they will go to be with Christ in heaven. But as this conviction grows in them, so, too, does an awareness that God has planned this all along. Even the apostle Paul, who persecuted the church before his conversion, came to understand that he had been prepared for salvation from the time he was born (Gal 1:15), and his experience is paradigmatic for believers.

Those who experience God's calling are greatly strengthened by the knowledge that he loves them and has saved them. They see him at work in their lives, suppressing the desire to sin and leading them into the kind of behavior that is pleasing to God. For them it is a great blessing and an encouragement to love him more and more. Unfortunately, those who have not had this experience may be persuaded that they have been rejected by God and so pass their time in sin, despairing of any hope of salvation. Predestination, by its nature, is a doctrine that only those who have experienced the saving grace of Christ can understand and appreciate as they should, and so the preaching ministry of the church must focus on bringing that experience to bear on everyone who hears the gospel. To do otherwise is to distort the teaching of Scripture and leads to error. Our task is not to speculate about who is (or is not) predestined, but to proclaim the way of salvation, and allow the Holy Spirit to bestow the assurance of election on those who respond positively to the message.

Anglicans do not take an official position on the fate of those who are not predestined to eternal life. These "reprobates," as they are known, are presumably condemned to eternal damnation, but this is not clearly stated in Scripture, and the article does not mention it. It seems logical that those who are not predestined to eternal life must be condemned to eternal damnation, and many Christians have drawn that conclusion, but Anglicans (at least officially) have hesitated to go that far. Human logic cannot fathom the depths of God, and in this case a dignified silence is preferable to speculation that may turn out to have been misplaced.

ARTICLE 18: OF OBTAINING ETERNAL
SALVATION ONLY BY THE NAME OF CHRIST

> They also are to be had accursed that presume to say,
> That every man shall be saved by the Law or Sect
> which he professeth, so that he be diligent to frame
> his life according to that Law, and the light of Nature.
> For Holy Scripture doth set out unto us only the
> Name of Jesus Christ, whereby men must be saved.

Anglicans do not believe that there is anyone who will be saved apart from Jesus Christ. Note that salvation is not dependent on belonging to the Church, but rather on confessing the name of Christ as Savior. This conviction is not a licence to disrespect people of other faiths or none, and Anglicans do not believe that anyone can be forcibly converted or coerced into the kingdom of heaven. But at the same time, we also do not believe that non-Christians can be saved by whatever beliefs they may have. Sincerity is not enough—there must also be conviction of truth, and the truth is found only in Jesus Christ.

This is an unpopular doctrine today, and many people are inclined to object to this article, but it is the teaching of Jesus in John 14:6, and the church's missionary work reflects its importance. Respect for the beliefs of others is essential, but agreeing with them is not. Christ is the only way to salvation, and we must proclaim that to everyone as an act of love. To fail to do this on the ground that other beliefs are equally valid is to deny the gospel and to discriminate against those who have not accepted it.

Christian exclusiveness is not meant to keep people out of heaven but to assure them that the salvation offered in Christ is the same for everyone. To assert that there may be other ways of getting to heaven is to open the door to comparisons that may be unhelpful and discriminate, however unintentionally, against others. If there are other ways to God, are they superior or inferior to the way proclaimed in and through Christ? Christians must have some reason for preferring him over other possible options, but is that saying (in effect) that other ways are less attractive or desirable, even if they may get people there in the end? Is it better to reach our destination by following a steep mountain track or by taking the superhighway that has been specially prepared for the same purpose? To change the metaphor, Christians want a level playing field for all who seek salvation, and that is what we have been offered (and what we offer to others) in Christ.

We may summarize this section on the Way of Salvation as follows:

1. All have sinned and come short of the glory of God.

2. Nobody can save themselves by their own efforts.

3. Human beings are justified before God only by faith in Jesus Christ.

4. Good works are important for believers but contribute nothing to our salvation.

5. Baptism does not take away sinfulness or make us perfect in the sight of God.

6. Christians come to a knowledge of salvation in time and space but then discover that they have been eternally predestined by God to dwell with him forever.

THE CHURCH

ARTICLE 19: OF THE CHURCH

> The visible Church of Christ is a congregation of
> faithful men, in the which the pure Word of God is
> preached, and the Sacraments be duly ministered
> according to Christ's ordinance in all those things
> that of necessity are requisite to the same.
>
> As the Church of *Jerusalem*, *Alexandria*, and
> *Antioch*, have erred; so also the Church of *Rome*
> hath erred, not only in their living and manner of
> Ceremonies, but also in matters of Faith.

Anglicans define the church as a gathering of believers
where the word of God is preached correctly and where
the sacraments are properly administered. The next article makes it clear that the word of God is Holy Scripture,
which suggests that by "pure" is meant "correctly interpreted." Anglicans make no claim to infallibility in these
matters, and reject the pretensions of those who do, though
it is probably true to say that the authors of this article
believed that the Church of England was as close to the
ideal as it was possible to get.

The listing of Jerusalem, Alexandria, and Antioch is that
of the ancient patriarchates of the East, which were generally
regarded as the supreme depositories of orthodox teaching.
(Constantinople, being of later origin, is not mentioned.)
Most important of all, however, is the insistence that fal-
libility applies to the Roman Church also, something that
Rome has always denied. On this point, no compromise is

possible, and Anglicans reject the idea that a doctrine or practice must be accepted merely because Rome has said so.

Applying this teaching in practice is more complicated than it may seem. By "visible Church" the article meant in the first instance the Church of England, whose teaching ministry and worship were supposed to conform to the will of Christ. Determining what that will is, however, turned out to be more difficult. For example, Anglicans decided that due administration of the sacraments included the retention of infant baptism, a belief that was contested at the time and is still rejected today, not only by Baptists but also by some Anglicans. Quite what preaching the "pure Word of God" means is also controversial. Presumably it was intended to indicate that all preaching should be based on an exposition of Holy Scripture, and that view is still held today, especially by evangelicals in the Anglican Communion. But many others have a much broader interpretation, and it is doubtful whether any consensus could be reached at the present time. Stated as it is, most Anglicans can accept this article, but its deeper implications are too vague and susceptible to different interpretations to make it readily applicable in today's Church.

It is significant that at this point we meet serious difficulties, not only in the relationship of Anglicans to others, but also within the Anglican Communion itself. Other differences certainly have their importance, but they are less closely tied to the institution of the visible church and the nature of its rituals and practices. Those who hold most firmly to this article tend to interpret it as an ideal that ought to be achieved rather than as a reality that can be clearly seen in Anglicanism, and few would be so bold as to claim that the Anglican Communion manifests all that is best in the visible church. In this, they are almost certainly at variance with the sixteenth-century Reformers, who thought that they had more or less achieved the ideal, and who would have been prepared to argue that case against all rivals. But if such convictions are now much less common than they once were, we should nevertheless accept that the wording of the article is flexible enough to allow it to serve as an ideal to be aimed for, rather than as a description of what the Reformation had achieved. To that extent, Anglican theology can be said to possess an inner adaptability that a more detailed confession of faith might be unable to match.

Article 20: Of the Authority of the Church

> The Church hath power to decree Rites or Ceremonies, and authority in Controversies of Faith: And yet it is not lawful for the Church to ordain any thing that is contrary to God's Word written, neither may it so expound one place of Scripture, that it be repugnant to another. Wherefore, although the Church be a witness and a keeper of Holy Writ, yet, as it ought not to decree any thing against the same, so besides the same ought it not to enforce any thing to be believed for necessity of Salvation.

This article states clearly that the Church is subject to Holy Scripture, which may be said to be its written constitution. The Church is free to order its worship and practice as it sees fit, provided that nothing it does goes against the teaching of the Bible. Nor is the Church permitted to interpret one passage of Scripture in a way that makes it contradict what the text as a whole teaches.

The first question that must be asked about this is what is meant by the word "Church." The context of the Articles makes it clear that, at a minimum, this will be the Church of England, but it says nothing about other churches around the world. No doubt the authors of the article would have expected the same standard to be applied in every local church, and we know from other texts (like the preface *Of Ceremonies* that was placed at the beginning of the 1549 Prayer Book) that Anglicans were prepared to accept a wide degree of variation in different national or local churches, but the possibility that all would (or might) come to a common mind is not excluded. Today, in the ecumenical climate of our times, it might be argued that interdenominational consensus in liturgical and other matters is greater than it has been at any time since the Reformation, and Anglicans have been willing participants in this, even as they retain the right to apply it in different ways according to local preferences and circumstances.

As with Article 19, the principles are easier to maintain in theory than they are to apply in practice. For a start, it is not stated how the Church decrees rites and ceremonies or exercises its authority. Is this the prerogative of its bishops, of a synod, or of an unspecified body representing the entire Anglican Communion? Nor is it clear what would be considered to be "contrary to God's Word written." Many would argue that same-sex marriage belongs in that category, but those who favor such innovations prefer to speak of the general sense of the Bible (for example, that God is love) and what they see as a trajectory of development that is still working itself out. The majority of Anglicans would see such interpretations as deceptive, to say the least, but at present it seems impossible for them to impose their view on the dissenting minority.

On the "chicken and egg" question of whether the church created the Scriptures or the other way around, Anglicans have avoided giving a clear answer. The church is described as a "witness and keeper" of the sacred text, which means that it has recognized which books belong in the canon and protects them from being distorted or lost. Those who wrote the texts were members of the church with special authority given to them by God, not by other Christians. The biblical canon thus emerged within the bosom of the church, but no ecclesiastical council or bishop commissioned its production. The New Testament canon emerged over time as orthodox preachers and teachers saw the Holy Spirit using particular books to further their ministry and edify the church. For a time there was hesitation over some of the writings, whose apostolic origins were unclear, but on the whole, there was a remarkable (and apparently spontaneous) consensus, at least from the fourth century onwards. The process of canonization extended over many centuries and was not complete until the sixteenth century, as witnessed in Article 6.

ARTICLE 21: OF THE AUTHORITY OF GENERAL COUNCILS

> General Councils may not be gathered together without the commandment and will of Princes. And when they be gathered together, (forasmuch as they be an assembly of men, whereof all be not governed with the Spirit and Word of God,) they may err, and

> sometimes have erred, even in things pertaining unto
> God. Wherefore things ordained by them as neces-
> sary to salvation have neither strength nor authority,
> unless it may be declared that they be taken out of
> Holy Scripture.

By "general councils," this article is referring primarily to
the ecumenical councils that had been summoned at different times in order to decide disputed questions of doctrine and practice. In ancient times, these councils had been
called together by the Roman emperor, though he himself
played no part in their deliberations. In the middle ages, it
was a matter of dispute as to whether such councils could
be summoned by the pope, acting as Christ's vicar on earth,
or whether the Byzantine or Holy Roman emperor had to
approve as well. This was still a living question when this
article was composed, because the Council of Trent (1545–
1563) had been summoned by the pope but could not meet
without imperial approval, which was only given on condition that the council should be held on imperial territory—at
Trent, rather than in Rome.

Today, circumstances have changed, and a general council could only be called by the different churches involved,
without state interference of any kind. But it must be remembered that in the sixteenth century, the "princes," not clergy
and bishops, represented the lay people. Anglicans have
always believed that a council of the whole Church must
have adequate lay representation, something which is not
accepted by Rome or by the Eastern churches, both of which
restrict participation to bishops.

As for the authority of church councils, they are subject
to the teaching of Scripture. If their decisions are not based

on the Bible, they cannot be enforced as being necessary for salvation, even if they are acceptable for practical purposes of church government. In particular, decisions taken at earlier councils cannot bind their successors, especially if it can be shown that they were taken in error, even if that error was the result of pardonable ignorance.

Anglicans do not formally recognize the decisions taken by Roman Catholic councils in modern times, though they have shown considerable interest in the proceedings of the Second Vatican Council (1962–1965), which is the most recent one to date. Nor do they feel bound by decisions taken by such bodies as the World Council of Churches, or even by the Primates' Meeting of the Anglican Communion, even if they respect them or even choose to adopt them.

Within England, the established status of the Church gives a certain relevance to this article, since it is impossible for the synods of the Church of England to convene or to legislate without the consent of Parliament, but elsewhere the separation of Church and state has made it a dead letter, and in the United States the Episcopal Church suppressed it as long ago as 1801. Nevertheless, the principle that councils may err and are therefore not definitive in matters of faith and doctrine remains a valid one, and most Anglicans would readily subscribe to it.

ARTICLE 22: OF PURGATORY

> The Romish Doctrine concerning Purgatory, Pardons, Worshipping, and Adoration, as well of Images as of Reliques, and also Invocation of Saints, is a fond thing vainly invented, and grounded upon no warranty of Scripture, but rather repugnant to the Word of God.

This article rejects not only the Roman doctrine of purgatory, but also many other devotional practices that have grown up and imposed themselves on the church without sufficient biblical warrant. Anglicans sometimes accept certain traditional practices, like calling prominent ancient and medieval Christians saints, but they reject the cult of such people as if they were especially holy or closer to God than anyone else. There is also no place in Anglican worship for the veneration of relics, something that smacks more of paganism than of the gospel of Christ. Nor do Anglicans venerate icons or canonize new "saints," though they have no objection to having pictures in churches and sometimes honor prominent church members who are believed to have made a lasting contribution to church life. A firm line is drawn between honor, which is acceptable, and veneration, which is not. For the most part, it must be said that things of this kind play only a peripheral role in Anglican life and are nowhere near as important as they are in the Roman Catholic or Eastern Orthodox churches.

It may be questioned by some as to whether this article belongs in a section on the church, but a read of Martin Luther's *Ninety-five Theses* will demonstrate why it does. One of Luther's main complaints against the papacy was its claim to be able to determine who was in purgatory and how much time they would have to spend there. Luther argued that the pope's assertion of jurisdiction over the afterlife was *ultra vires*, but of course it was based on the belief that the church is not confined to this world. As long as a soul was not in heaven, it was held to be subject to the papacy in some form or other, and so purgatory was an extension of the church militant here on earth—a claim that Anglicans rejected, along with the doctrine of purgatory itself.

This section on the church may be summed up as follows:

1. A true church is one that preaches the pure Word of God and administers the sacraments in the right way.

2. All existing churches have fallen into error.

3. No church can decree anything contrary to, or not contained in, Holy Scripture.

THE MINISTRY

There are only two articles that deal specifically with the ordained ministry, though several others, particularly those on the sacraments, contain provisions that supplement what is expressed here. The articles are neatly divided into how a minister is appointed and how he is expected to exercise his ministry in the Church. Neither is particularly controversial today, though there are still some ecclesial bodies that do not conform to the standards laid down by these articles, and whose ministers (and ministries) fall short of Anglican principles, making it difficult for Anglicans to enter into closer relations with them.

Article 23: Of Ministering in the Congregation

> It is not lawful for any man to take upon him the office of publick preaching, or ministering the Sacraments in the Congregation, before he be lawfully called, and sent to execute the same. And those we ought to judge lawfully called and sent, which be chosen and called to this work by men who have publick authority given unto them in the

> Congregation, to call and send Ministers into the
> Lord's vineyard.

This article governs the appointment of ministers in the
Church, who must follow a procedure set by the relevant
authorities. Note that the article says nothing about episcopal ordination, which was not made compulsory in the
Church of England until 1660, and then for political reasons. The intention of the article is to ensure what we
would now call quality control. Congregations have a right
to expect that their ministers will be able to perform the
tasks entrusted to them, and it is the duty of the Church
to provide adequate means for selecting and training suitable candidates.

Today it is typically assumed that candidates for ministry
will have (or acquire) a theological training, usually based
in a college or dispensed by means of a course that covers
the basic requirements. This is widely practiced across the
Christian world, but by the standards of other churches,
Anglican ministerial training is often regarded as inferior,
with relatively little emphasis on theology. It is certainly true
that standards have declined in the past generation and that,
in many places, Anglican clergy are not fully equipped for
the ministry to which they have been called. The responsibility for this must lie with the Church authorities, who have
acquiesced in this situation for financial reasons as much as
anything else. The principles laid down in this article are
clear and are generally agreed by almost everybody, but the
practice is left wanting and needs to be urgently addressed,
not least in the developed world, where the resources are
plentiful but the willingness to make proper use of them is
less obvious.

ARTICLE 24: OF SPEAKING IN THE CONGREGATION IN SUCH A TONGUE AS THE PEOPLE UNDERSTANDETH

> It is a thing plainly repugnant to the Word of God, and the custom of the Primitive Church, to have publick Prayer in the Church, or to minister the Sacraments, in a tongue not understanded of the people.

This article is uncontroversial nowadays and would probably not be included in a modern confession of faith, but it was written against the background of more than one thousand years when church services were conducted in Latin and few people could understand them. Today, it is only in some Eastern churches that ancient forms of language are still regularly used in the liturgy. Note that the article does not specify that worship should be conducted in the mother tongue of the congregation. There are places in the world today where multi-ethnic congregations worship in a common language (often English) that is universally understood but is not the native language of most church members. Anglicans accept that reality and do not try to split congregations along linguistic lines unless that is necessary for communication purposes.

These articles are easily summed up as follows:

1. Ministry in the Church ought to be properly regulated.
2. Ministry in the Church ought to be understood by those who receive it.

THE SACRAMENTS

ARTICLE 25: OF THE SACRAMENTS

Sacraments ordained of Christ be not only badges or tokens of Christian men's profession, but rather they be certain sure witnesses, and effectual signs of grace, and God's good will towards us, by the which he doth work invisibly in us, and doth not only quicken, but also strengthen and confirm our Faith in him.

There are two Sacraments ordained of Christ our Lord in the Gospel, that is to say, Baptism, and the Supper of the Lord.

Those five commonly called Sacraments, that is to say, Confirmation, Penance, Orders, Matrimony, and extreme Unction, are not to be counted for Sacraments of the Gospel, being such as have grown partly of the corrupt following of the Apostles, partly are states of life allowed in the Scriptures; but yet have not like nature of Sacraments with Baptism, and the Lord's Supper, for that they have not any visible sign or ceremony ordained of God.

The Sacraments were not ordained of Christ to be gazed upon, or to be carried about, but that we should duly use them. And in such only as worthily receive the same they have a wholesome effect or operation: but they that receive them unworthily purchase to themselves damnation, as Saint *Paul* saith.

The Anglican doctrine of the sacraments closely resembles the teaching of John Calvin in his *Institutes of the Christian Religion*. They are more than simply signs of a faith already professed, but they have no power to implant faith in a person who does not have it. Rather, the sacraments bear witness to God's saving grace and strengthen our faith in him by reminding us that the gospel is not just an idea in the mind but a life-transforming experience that affects every part of our being.

Only baptism and the Lord's Supper are true sacraments because only they bear witness to the saving power of Christ's gospel. The medieval church had developed a sacramental system by which there were seven rites that qualified as means of grace, but Anglicans reject this scheme. Confirmation is not really a sacrament because it is the completion of baptism, penance is a ritual divorced from the repentance it is supposed to signify, orders are administrative procedures within the church that do not convey any special grace to those who receive them, matrimony is much broader than the church, and extreme unction is a misapplication of James 5:14–15, where the anointing is meant for healing and not as a preparation for death.

Anglicans also reject the devotional practices that grew up around the sacraments (particularly the Lord's Supper) in the middle ages. The sacraments are meant to be used, not venerated. Those who receive them worthily benefit from their purpose, but those who partake of them unworthily condemn themselves, as Paul says in 1 Corinthians 11:27–30. This condemnation must be understood in a spiritual sense. There is no reason to suppose that those who abuse the sacraments will necessarily be struck down by disease or some other misfortune, because the sacramental elements are not like drugs that have power in themselves to cause harm. Rather, misuse of the means of grace is dangerous because it leads to a misunderstanding of the way God works and therefore compromises the recipient's ability to discern what is spiritually profitable from what is not.

The article's emphasis on the danger of unworthy reception must be noted because it presumes that such reception is possible, which it would not be if the sacraments were capable of implanting the grace to which they bear witness. It is clear from this warning that the recipient must be properly prepared to benefit from the sacraments, though the article does not specify what that preparation consists of. From the rites as they are set out in the *Book of Common Prayer*, we can deduce that they must be received by faith. In the case of the Lord's Supper, it is the faith of the communicant himself or herself that is required. In the case of baptism, it is the faith of the person being baptized (if an adult) or the faith of his or her parents or sponsors, which the recipient must then confirm when he or she is of an age to do so.

ARTICLE 26: OF THE UNWORTHINESS OF THE MINISTERS, WHICH HINDERS NOT THE EFFECT OF THE SACRAMENT

> Although in the visible Church the evil be ever mingled with the good, and sometimes the evil have chief authority in the Ministration of the Word and Sacraments, yet forasmuch as they do not the same in their own name, but in Christ's, and do minister by his commission and authority, we may use their Ministry, both in hearing the Word of God, and in receiving of the Sacraments. Neither is the effect of Christ's ordinance taken away by their wickedness, nor the grace of God's gifts diminished from such as by faith and rightly do receive the Sacraments

ministered unto them; which be effectual, because
of Christ's institution and promise, although they be
ministered by evil men.

Nevertheless, it apperteineth to the discipline of
the Church, that inquiry be made of evil Ministers,
and that they be accused by those that have knowledge of their offences; and finally being found guilty,
by just judgment be deposed.

Anglicans believe that the ministry of the Church is greater
than any individual minister, and therefore state that the
work of an unworthy minister is not discredited by that fact
alone. If it were, no ministry would be valid, because all have
sinned and come short of the glory of God. The validity of
a sacrament does not lie in the spiritual state of the minister,
which is usually unknown and probably unknowable, but in
the promises that the sacrament contains. Christ instituted
baptism and the Lord's Supper as demonstrations of the
preaching of the gospel of salvation. They have no meaning
apart from that preaching and will have no effect if they are
not received by faith.

It is important to distinguish between the objective content of the sacraments and their subjective administration by
(and to) sinful people. Because the minister is only the agent
of the sacraments, he cannot add to them by any spiritual
power present in himself, nor can his own spiritual state
before God subtract from their efficacy.

At the same time, the Church has a duty to maintain
high standards in its ministry, and if some of those in holy
orders have shown themselves to be unworthy of the tasks
assigned to them, it is the duty of the authorities to exercise
discipline and depose them. This is particularly important

nowadays, when the media have exposed scandals among the clergy that have not been properly addressed. There is no excuse for laxity in this respect, and the Church must intervene to protect its members and its activities from abuses caused by ministers who have betrayed their trust. Most Anglican churches have disciplinary procedures for dealing with problems of this kind, though their effectiveness has sometimes been questioned. Nevertheless, it is the principle that counts as a matter of doctrine, and Anglicans have always been conscious of the need to exercise discipline among the clergy, which is one of the main functions of the bishops.

ARTICLE 27: OF BAPTISM

> Baptism is not only a sign of profession, and mark of difference, whereby Christian men are discerned from others that be not christened, but it is also a sign of Regeneration or new Birth, whereby, as by an instrument, they that receive Baptism rightly are grafted into the Church; the promises of forgiveness of sin, and of our adoption to be the sons of God by the Holy Ghost, are visibly signed and sealed; Faith is confirmed, and Grace increased by virtue of prayer unto God. The Baptism of young Children is in any wise to be retained in the Church, as most agreeable with the institution of Christ.

Baptism is not just a sign of a Christian's distinctiveness, like circumcision among the Jews, but also of new life in Christ. Those who receive it in faith are made members of the church and receive the gospel promises of forgiveness and adoption by the Holy Spirit as children of God. The Roman Catholic Church teaches that those who are baptized are born again by the infusion of sacramental grace, but Anglicans reject that and do not teach baptismal regeneration, as this doctrine is called. Baptism is the outward and visible sign of an inward and spiritual grace, but the external rite cannot produce the spiritual transformation that it represents.

The rejection of baptismal regeneration was determined in 1850 in what is known as the Gorham judgment. George Cornelius Gorham (1787–1857) was refused institution to a benefice by the bishop of Exeter, on the ground that Gorham did not believe in baptismal regeneration. The case went to the judicial committee of the privy council, which ruled that Gorham was correct in denying that the Church of England taught that doctrine. A few high churchmen left the Church as a result and became Roman Catholics, but the decision has never been contested or reversed. At stake is the relationship between the sign (baptism) and the thing signified (regeneration). The article specifies only those who *rightly* receive baptism benefit from the grace it signifies, and of course it is impossible to determine that objectively. It is certain that many baptized people have never shown any sign of the grace of God at work in their lives, and some have even repudiated the notion and abandoned the Christian faith altogether.

Anglicans practice infant baptism on the ground that it is compatible with the intention of Jesus when he instituted the sacrament. This can only mean that Jesus saw it as the sign of a promise given to those who would receive it by faith, whether they were aware of it at the time or not. For some

Anglicans today, infant baptism is a dubious practice and they prefer not to follow it, but ministers of the Church must offer it to those who desire it for their children. Anglicans do not condemn or seek to discipline church members who reject infant baptism, nor do they insist on sprinkling as opposed to immersion, or vice versa. It is fair to say that infant baptism is the norm in Anglican churches, but that Anglicans are generally tolerant of the views of others. At the same time, they recognize the validity of infant baptism and would not baptize someone twice.

Many people believe that there is a parallel between New Testament baptism and Old Testament circumcision, in the sense that both are initiations into—and promise the blessings of—the covenant that God has made with his people and that has been fulfilled in Christ. But just as there were many Israelites who were circumcised outwardly without being true children of God (Rom 9:3–8), so there are many people today who receive water baptism outwardly but who remain untouched by the Holy Spirit and never profess faith as Christians.

ARTICLE 28: OF THE LORD'S SUPPER

> The Supper of the Lord is not only a sign of the love
> that Christians ought to have among themselves
> one to another; but rather is a Sacrament of our
> Redemption by Christ's death: insomuch that to such
> as rightly, worthily, and with faith, receive the same,
> the Bread which we break is a partaking of the Body
> of Christ; and likewise the Cup of Blessing is a par-
> taking of the Blood of Christ.

Transubstantiation (or the change of the substance of Bread and Wine) in the Supper of the Lord, cannot be proved by Holy Writ; but is repugnant to the plain words of Scripture, overthroweth the nature of a Sacrament, and hath given occasion to many superstitions.

The Body of Christ is given, taken, and eaten, in the Supper, only after an heavenly and spiritual manner. And the mean whereby the Body of Christ is received and eaten in the Supper is Faith.

The Sacrament of the Lord's Supper was not by Christ's ordinance reserved, carried about, lifted up, or worshipped.

The Lord's Supper is not just a fellowship meal but a sign of our salvation by the death of Christ. As with baptism, it is effective only in those who receive it rightly. These principles undergird the Anglican doctrine of the Lord's Supper and must be considered together. On the one hand, it is a fellowship meal in which all baptized Christians are invited to participate. There is no fixed minimum number of communicants (though it is usually held to be three, including the celebrant), but purely private celebrations, such as can occur in the Roman Catholic Church, are ruled out. So too, one must assume, are celebrations intentionally reserved for specific groups of people to the exclusion of other Christians—all of God's people are welcome at the Lord's table.

At the same time, Christian fellowship is not social friendliness but a communion in the atoning death and resurrection of Christ. It is his atonement that the Supper commemorates, and his broken body and poured-out blood that unite us to him by paying the price for our sins.

These two dimensions of the Lord's Supper must be held together, because each is necessary in itself and complements the other. In recent years there has been a tendency among liturgists to emphasize fellowship at the expense of atonement, perhaps in reaction to the opposite tendency in the past, and bias in one direction or the other is a constant danger. It must be avoided, since to distort the Lord's Supper is to distort the gospel and weaken the faith of those who are meant to be strengthened by it.

The medieval doctrine of transubstantiation was based on an Aristotelian theory of matter, according to which things could be analyzed in terms of substance and accidents (weight, color, etc.). In the Lord's Supper, so went the theory, the accidents of bread and wine remain the same, but their underlying substances are miraculously transformed into the body and blood of Christ. With the abandonment of Aristotle's physics, this doctrine is now untenable in its original form, and modern Roman Catholic theologians are often at a loss as to how to interpret it in a way that makes sense today. Anglicans are not troubled by this difficulty, because they have always rejected the doctrine, and it is perhaps here more than anywhere else that the distance between Rome and the Anglican Communion can most clearly be measured.

Anglicans have always rejected the doctrine of transubstantiation on the ground that it makes no sense and that it distorts what a sacrament is. Just as a wedding ring is not a marriage, so the elements of the Lord's Supper are not in themselves the body and blood of Christ. Sacraments represent the things they signify, but they are outward and visible signs of an inward and spiritual grace, and not that grace itself.

Anglicans therefore reject the devotional exercises that surrounded the consecrated elements in medieval times, partly because those exercises presuppose that they have become Christ's body and blood (which the *Articles of Religion* deny) and partly because Christ never authorized such practices. Improper devotion is not a matter of indifference because it can easily lead to error and cut people off from the very gift they are supposed to be receiving.

ARTICLE 29: OF THE WICKED WHICH EAT NOT THE BODY OF CHRIST IN THE USE OF THE LORD'S SUPPER

> The Wicked, and such as be void of a lively faith, although they do carnally and visibly press with their teeth (as Saint *Augustine* saith) the Sacrament of the Body and Blood of Christ, yet in no wise are they partakers of Christ: but rather, to their condemnation, do eat and drink the sign or Sacrament of so great a thing.

This article was struck out by Queen Elizabeth I in 1563, on the ground that it might offend the Lutherans. However, it was reinstated in 1571, and, as a result, the Lutheran Formula of Concord (1577) anathematized Anglicans along with other Reformed Protestants who shared their view. Lutherans have traditionally believed that the body of Christ is present in the Lord's Supper "in, with and under" the consecrated elements, but the Reformed reject that idea. Flesh and blood can eat and drink material things like bread and wine, which correspond with them, but are unable to partake of spiritual things. The efficacy of the sacrament, however, depends on faith, and it is only those who possess faith who share in it. Everyone else eats and drinks to their own condemnation because they fail to respect the significance of the sacramental act. As in the other articles in this section, the sign is distinct from the thing signified and has no power independent of it.

Article 30: Of both Kinds

The Cup of the Lord is not to be denied to the Laypeople: for both the parts of the Lord's Sacrament, by Christ's ordinance and commandment, ought to be ministered to all Christian men alike.

This article insists that communicants must partake of both the bread and wine, as Christ intended. It is included here because in 1415 the Council of Constance ruled that communicants need receive only the bread, on the ground that the blood is included in the body. In traditional Roman Catholic teaching, the celebrant drinks of the cup as the representative of the people, a role which Anglicans do not attribute to him because no human being can come between a believer and God. The question was hotly debated in the late fourteenth and early fifteenth centuries, especially in Bohemia, where there was an important Utraquist movement, so called because of its insistence on Communion "in both kinds" (*sub utraque specie*). Its champion Jan Hus was

summoned to the Council of Constance (Konstanz), condemned as a heretic and burnt at the stake, despite a safe
conduct that had been issued to him by the Holy Roman
emperor. Martin Luther regarded himself as standing in
the tradition of Hus, and so this article has strong under-
tones of Protestant opposition to Rome. The underlying
issue was the authority of the church *versus* the plain witness of the Bible. It is clear that New Testament celebrations of the Lord's Supper always involved Communion in
both kinds, but the medieval church claimed the authority to overrule that. Today, it may be said, many Roman
Catholics do receive Communion in both kinds, and most
would probably agree that the problem should never have
arisen in the first place.

There may be circumstances related to health issues in
which a communicant is unable to receive the cup, and if
that is so, Communion in one kind is not invalid. But that
is not the same thing as deliberately withholding the cup
from communicants for some spurious theological reason.
In normal circumstances, the bread and the wine are meant
to be consumed together by every communicant, as the
teaching of Christ in the New Testament clearly indicates.

It should be said that Anglicans do not specify what kind
of bread or wine should be used at the Lord's Supper. Should
the bread be leavened or unleavened (as it was in the Last
Supper of Jesus)? Should the wine be fermented or not? As
far as Anglicans are concerned, these are matters that can
be decided according to circumstances and do not have any
doctrinal significance. That is now the view adopted by most
other churches as well, though for many centuries there
were debates between the Western and Eastern churches

about whether leavened or unleavened bread should be used, the West preferring unleavened bread and the East objecting that this was a Jewish practice! Some Anglicans prefer (unleavened) wafers to (leavened) bread, but this is a local choice and has no theological implications.

Among other Protestants, there is occasionally some debate about whether to use fermented or unfermented wine, but this seems to have arisen from the temperance (anti-alcohol) movements of the late nineteenth and early twentieth centuries, not from any theological concerns.

ARTICLE 31: OF THE ONE OBLATION OF CHRIST FINISHED UPON THE CROSS

> The Offering of Christ once made is that perfect redemption, propitiation, and satisfaction, for all the sins of the whole world, both original and actual; and there is none other satisfaction for sin, but that alone. Wherefore the sacrifices of Masses, in the which it was commonly said, that the Priest did offer Christ for the quick and the dead, to have remission of pain or guilt, were blasphemous fables, and dangerous deceits.

The Lord's Supper is a memorial of the atoning sacrifice of Christ, which was made once for all on the cross. The medieval doctrine that the celebrating priest somehow brought Christ's sacrifice back to earth by transubstantiating the consecrated bread and wine is rejected by Anglicans. So, too, is the Catholic practice of offering masses for the benefit of both the living and the dead, which Anglicans regard as false and even blasphemous. The purpose of the Lord's Supper is to set out the death of Christ as the one sufficient sacrifice for sin, not to copy or repeat it in some way.

The language of this article is duplicated and expanded in the Prayer of Consecration used at Holy Communion, where it is designed to impress upon those who are about to receive the sacramental elements the true nature of a sacrament. Given the generally moderate tone of most of the articles, it is remarkable how violent the language here appears to be. The English Reformers were clearly exercised by what they saw as anti-Christian practices associated with the Eucharist in the Roman Catholic Church. Nowadays, of course, ecumenical dialogue demands a more temperate approach to these questions, but the underlying issues have not gone away, and modern Anglicans need to remember the strength of feeling against these practices that there was during the Reformation.

ARTICLE 32: OF THE MARRIAGE OF PRIESTS

> Bishops, Priests, and Deacons, are not commanded by God's Law, either to vow the estate of single life, or to abstain from marriage: therefore it is lawful for them, as for all other Christian men, to marry at their own discretion, as they shall judge the same to serve better to godliness.

Anglicans reject the Catholic view that those in bishop's and priest's orders must submit to a discipline of perpetual celibacy. The Roman Catholic Church will ordain married men as deacons, but not normally as priests or bishops, though this prohibition is not a matter of doctrine but of discipline. The Eastern Orthodox churches will ordain married men as priests, but not as bishops, and a priest whose wife dies must remain celibate. Anglicans have always accepted the legitimacy of clerical marriage, which they leave to the discretion of those involved. Marriage is not a sacrament but a civil ordinance that is open to all who are capable of it, but it is not to be forced on anyone. Priests and bishops are not to be regarded as distinct social orders, and so the same rules apply to them as to every other Church member.

The purpose of clerical marriage is to promote godliness, and it has to be said that there is sufficient evidence of scandal among the supposedly celibate Catholic clergy to make this more than just a pious wish. Of course, married clergy are not exempt from the demand for personal holiness, and Anglicans have frequently debated whether a divorced person ought to continue in ordained ministry, particularly if he or she chooses to remarry within the lifetime of the previous spouse.

It hardly needs to be said that the English Reformers never envisaged same-sex marriage, which is specifically excluded by the order for Holy Matrimony in the *Book of Common Prayer*, though recently some Anglican churches have either ordained people in that situation or allowed clergy to enter into such unions. In fact, this is now the chief bone of contention that threatens to divide the Anglican world, a circumstance that would have shocked the Reformers, but that makes us realize just how important our understanding of matrimony is for the welfare of the church as a whole.

ARTICLE 33: OF EXCOMMUNICATE PERSONS, HOW THEY ARE TO BE AVOIDED

> That person which by open denunciation of the Church is rightly cut off from the unity of the Church, and excommunicated, ought to be taken of the whole multitude of the faithful, as a Heathen and Publican, until he be openly reconciled by penance, and received into the Church by a Judge that hath authority thereunto.

Anglicans believe that the Church has the right to discipline, by excluding them from the fellowship, members who have openly rejected or betrayed the faith. This exclusion is not intended to be permanent, and where there is suitable repentance, the guilty parties may be readmitted to Communion. In practice, this article is mostly a dead letter nowadays, but the Church continues to claim the right to exercise discipline over its erring members if that should be necessary. However, even in the most extreme cases, it is no longer true to say that those so disciplined are treated like "heathens and publicans." Shunning of that kind is still practiced by some small Protestant groups, but it is virtually unknown among Anglicans and would probably be regarded as both cruel and counterproductive.

It should be said that the *Book of Common Prayer* recognizes the difficulty of upholding biblical standards of discipline and says so in the service of Commination, which is meant to be used on Ash Wednesday. That does not make it any easier to apply those standards in the life of the church, but the existence of this article is a reminder of the claim that the church must make to discipline its members, however hard that may be in practice.

The section on the sacraments may be summed up as follows:

1. There are two sacraments of the gospel, baptism and the Lord's Supper.

2. The sacraments are outward and visible signs of an inner and spiritual grace.

3. Right reception of the sacraments is essential for them to be effective.

4. The Lord's Supper has frequently been abused, and these abuses must be eliminated.

5. The sacraments retain their validity even if those who administer them are unworthy.

6. The church must always seek to discipline its members, both clerical and lay, so that they reflect the status and ministry to which they have been called.

· 4 ·

The Local Articles and Matters Indifferent

(Articles 34–37)

T he English Reformers believed that each local Church had the right to legislate for itself on matters that in theological terms were regarded as "indifferent" (*adia-phora*). This was an important theological principle and has remained central to Anglicanism as it has spread across the world. Individual Anglican provinces were (and still are) free to order their internal affairs according to local circum-stances and traditions, and these articles set out what the Church of England considered the most important of them.

It should be said that the English Reformers interpreted the notion of a local or national church in political terms corresponding to what we would now call the state or the nation. Thus, the Church of England, which consists of two provinces (Canterbury and York) was a single local church. The Church of Ireland, which had four provinces (Armagh, Cashel, Dublin and Tuam) was also a single local church, but because Ireland was a kingdom annexed to the English crown, it was expected to follow the lead of the Church of England, and in the seventeenth century its freedom to act

independently was contested by William Laud, archbishop
of Canterbury (1633–1645).

On the other hand, for a long time the Church of England
made no attempt to establish itself in other Christian countries. Instead, it recognized the national churches there as
legitimate and sought to enter into relations with them as
much as it could. There was no concept of Anglicanism as a
distinct form of Christianity that ought to be spread to other
places, and when Anglicans ventured outside the British
Isles, it was as colonists and settlers, not as missionaries to
foreign peoples. It was only much later, in the nineteenth
century, that such missionary work began in earnest, and
even now there are no Anglican churches in continental
Europe, apart from English-speaking chaplaincies that serve
an essentially expatriate community. In the lands of sixteenth-
century Christendom, Anglicanism is still distinctly English
and seems likely to remain so for the foreseeable future.

ARTICLE 34: OF THE TRADITIONS OF THE CHURCH

> It is not necessary that Traditions and Ceremonies be
> in all places one, and utterly like; for at all times they
> have been divers, and may be changed according
> to the diversity of countries, times, and men's man-
> ners, so that nothing be ordained against God's Word.
> Whosoever through his private judgement, willingly
> and purposely, doth openly break the traditions and
> ceremonies of the Church, which be not repugnant to
> the Word of God, and be ordained and approved by
> common authority, ought to be rebuked openly, (that

others may fear to do the like,) as he that offendeth against the common order of the Church, and hurteth the authority of the Magistrate, and woundeth the consciences of the weak brethren.

Every particular or national Church hath authority to ordain, change, and abolish, ceremonies or rites of the Church ordained only by man's authority, so that all things be done to edifying.

Anglicans allow that autonomous national and local churches have the freedom to adopt patterns of worship that seem suitable to them, as long as they do not contradict anything found in Holy Scripture. At the same time, members of particular churches are expected to accept the patterns that their churches have adopted, even if they have no specific biblical warrant. This is for the sake of order within the Anglican Church, which must be preserved. The English Reformers believed that it was right to appeal to the civil magistrate in cases of disobedience, though nobody would do that nowadays. Even so, Anglicans still expect church members to stay within the bounds of discipline and practice that the local (national) church has deemed appropriate, whether they personally agree with the pattern adopted or not.

It is safe to say that modern Anglicans are generally very open-minded on this score. There is a wide variety of different practices that the Church tolerates and effectively encourages, even if it does not explicitly say so. In fact, Anglicans are now one of the most diverse denominations in this respect, not only between different national churches but also within them—and even in the same congregation.

In some places there is a strong emphasis on change and innovation, making it difficult to speak of traditions at all, though most Anglicans adhere to a pattern of Prayer Book worship that is easily recognizable around the world.

The downside of this tolerance is that Anglicans are loath to accept the coexistence of two or more Anglican churches in the same geographical area. In continental Europe this happens by accident, since the diocese of Europe, which is an integral part of the Church of England, does not compete with local national churches in Spain and Portugal, which have become Anglican in recent years, or with the American Episcopal churches in Europe. But it has created real difficulties in North America, South Africa, and elsewhere, where local Anglican churches have divided over various doctrinal matters and sought recognition from the worldwide Anglican Communion. Whether such recognition can be granted, or whether the "territorial principle" must be upheld (and thus effectively regarded as doctrine) is an unresolved question currently facing Anglicans.

ARTICLE 35: OF THE HOMILIES

> The second Book of Homilies, the several titles whereof we have joined under this Article, doth contain a godly and wholesome Doctrine, and necessary for these times, as doth the former Book of Homilies, which were set forth in the time of Edward the Sixth; and therefore we judge them to be read in Churches by the Ministers, diligently and distinctly, that they may be understanded of the people.
>
> Of the Names of the Homilies

1. Of the right Use of the Church.
2. Against peril of Idolatry.
3. Of repairing and keeping clean of Churches.
4. Of good Works: first of Fasting.
5. Against Gluttony and Drunkenness.
6. Against Excess of Apparel.
7. Of Prayer.
8. Of the Place and Time of Prayer.
9. That Common Prayers and Sacraments ought to be ministered in a known tongue.
10. Of the reverend estimation of God's Word.
11. Of Alms-doing.
12. Of the Nativity of Christ.
13. Of the Passion of Christ.
14. Of the Resurrection of Christ.
15. Of the worthy receiving of the Sacrament of the Body and Blood of Christ.
16. Of the Gifts of the Holy Ghost.
17. For the Rogation-days.
18. Of the State of Matrimony.
19. Of Repentance.
20. Against Idleness.
21. Against Rebellion.

The two books of Homilies are part of the doctrinal foundations of the Church of England. The first book was published in 1547, some years before the Articles made their appearance, and the Articles are to some extent a précis of them. There are twelve homilies in all, divided equally into doctrinal and moral subjects. The six homilies on doctrine are particularly important. Four of them were written by Archbishop Thomas Cranmer, and the other two by high churchmen—the second one on sin and the fall by John Harpsfield, and the sixth one on love by Edmund Bonner, bishop of London. The first homily is one of the best expositions of the nature of Holy Scripture ever written, and is particularly useful for understanding the Anglican approach to the sacred texts and the way they have been adapted for liturgical use in the *Book of Common Prayer*. The other three homilies outline the way of salvation, and the third one on justification by faith is specifically mentioned in Article 11 as a fuller explanation of the doctrine than what can be found in the article itself.

The second book appeared in 1563, at the same time as the revision of the Articles, and it was slightly modified in 1571 by the addition of lengthy homily against rebellion. As the titles indicate, the subject matter tends to focus more on personal behavior and on the Church's liturgical year than the first book does. It is also three times longer than the first book, and most of the homilies it contains are subdivided so that they could be read over several Sundays. In the sixteenth century, non-preaching ministers were expected to read them to their congregations, but that practice gradually died out, and today they are little known or studied. Nevertheless, they can still be used as source material for Anglican doctrine on subjects not covered elsewhere, and they are occasionally cited in official reports that treat a subject they cover.

The *Homilies* are especially important in that they indicate how preaching is meant to function as a means of conveying the Church's doctrine to its congregations. Following what the apostle Paul says in Romans 10, the English Reformers were convinced that faith comes by the faithful preaching of the word of God, and they made it central to their evangelistic activity. Even today, preaching remains central to Anglican worship, even to the celebration of the Eucharist, which should always begin with a reading of Holy Scripture, followed by a sermon expounding it to those intending to receive Communion.

ARTICLE 36: OF CONSECRATION OF BISHOPS AND MINISTERS

> The Book of Consecration of Archbishops and Bishops, and Ordering of Priests and Deacons, lately set forth in the time of *Edward* the Sixth, and confirmed at the same time by authority of Parliament, doth contain all things necessary to such Consecration and Ordering: neither hath it any thing, that of itself is superstitious or ungodly. And therefore whosoever are consecrated or ordered according to the Rites of that Book, since the second year of the aforenamed King *Edward* unto this time, or hereafter shall be consecrated or ordered according to the same Rites; we decree all such to be rightly, orderly, and lawfully consecrated and ordered.

This article makes the Ordinal, which was attached to the first *Book of Common Prayer* in 1549, the standard form of ordination to the ministry of the Church of England. It contains three separate rites, one for the consecration of bishops, one for the ordination of priests (presbyters), and one for the making of deacons. The Ordinal expounds the duties of all three and remains the template for Anglicans worldwide. In 1896, the Roman Catholic Church decreed that the Anglican Ordinal was "defective" because it does not give ministers the power to transubstantiate the sacramental elements, and so it declared Anglican orders null and void. The Eastern Orthodox churches do not recognize Anglican orders either, but they are more nuanced in their criticisms and have not rejected the Ordinal as such. Other churches recognize Anglican orders to varying degrees, according to their own criteria. For some, the ordination of women in many Anglican churches has made recognition more difficult, if not impossible, and this situation is unlikely to change in the foreseeable future.

Anglicans have no problem recognizing the orders of other episcopal churches and usually do so without difficulty. The status of non-episcopally ordained clergy is more problematic. Until the nineteenth century, there were times when Anglicans admitted men from non-episcopal churches into their ministry, but the Lambeth Conference of 1888 made episcopacy one of the four pillars of Anglicanism, and since then that practice has largely ceased. In recent years, however, the spirit of ecumenism has opened up the subject again, and there are now cases where Anglicans recognize non-episcopally ordained ministers in the context of local ecumenical projects. The current situation is more fluid than it used to be, and the prospects for the reunion of Anglicans and other Protestants are now higher than they were until quite recently. As far as the Roman Catholic and Eastern Orthodox churches are concerned, there has been no change.

The Ordinal claims that the three orders of ministry go back to the New Testament, but modern scholarship has called this into question, and Anglicans no longer put much emphasis on it. Today it is generally recognized that there is no real difference between bishops and presbyters (priests), who constituted a single order of ministry in the early church. Some efforts have been made to revive a permanent diaconate, which is now mainly a stepping stone to the presbyterate, but these have had only limited success. Many Anglican churches now ordain women as well as men, but those who do not are free not to recognize ordained women from other provinces. There is also considerable resistance to the ordination of practicing homosexuals, which has occurred in a few provinces but has been rejected by the majority. It has to be said, therefore, that ordained Anglican ministry is no longer uniform to the extent that it once was, although division focuses around the suitability of the candidates and not the nature of the ministry to which they are, have been, or will be ordained.

ARTICLE 37: OF THE CIVIL MAGISTRATES

The King's Majesty hath the chief power in this Realm of *England*, and other his Dominions, unto whom the chief Government of all Estates of this Realm, whether they be Ecclesiastical or Civil, in all causes doth appertain, and is not, nor ought to be, subject to any foreign Jurisdiction.

Where we attribute to the King's Majesty the chief government, by which Titles we understand the minds of some slanderous folks to be offended; we give not to our Princes the ministering either of God's Word, or of the Sacraments, the which thing the Injunctions also lately set forth by *Elizabeth* our Queen do most plainly testify; but that only prerogative, which we see to have been given always to all godly princes in Holy Scriptures by God himself; that is, that they should rule all estates and degrees committed to their charge by God, whether they be Ecclesiastical or Temporal, and restrain with the civil sword the stubborn and evil-doers.

The Bishop of *Rome* hath no jurisdiction in this Realm of *England*.

> The Laws of the Realm may punish Christian men with death, for heinous and grievous offences.
>
> It is lawful for Christian men, at the commandment of the Magistrate, to wear weapons, and to serve in the wars.

The Church of England recognises the sovereignty of the state in civil affairs, but it does not allow it to determine the nature or functions of its ministry. To give an example, the state cannot order the Church to ordain women if it chooses not to do so, nor can it oblige the Church to marry divorced people or perform same-sex weddings against its will. Church and state support one another, but each has its own sphere of competence in which it is sovereign. At the same time, Anglicans recognize that the clergy are not above the laws of the state and that if they break them, the state has every right to punish them on the same basis as all other citizens. However, the Church of England (unlike most other Anglican churches) still possesses ecclesiastical courts that are independent of the state's jurisdiction and that can be used for handling internal church matters, including clergy discipline.

This article repudiates the claims of the pope to universal jurisdiction, and thus constitutes a bar to reunion with the Church of Rome. It also allows that the state has the power to execute Church members, as well as to conscript them into the armed forces. In practice, most Anglicans are now against the death penalty and in favor of allowing conscientious objections to military service, but they advocate these policies as private citizens and do not pit the authority of the Church against that of the state.

It should be said in passing that this article says nothing about the establishment of the Church of England and does not claim that state officials ought to belong to it. The position of the monarch as Supreme Governor of the Church of England is regulated by the state, not by the Church, and it was not until the Act of Succession in 1701 that the reigning sovereign was obliged by law to be a communicant member of the Church. If the Church of England is ever disestablished, that requirement will doubtless lapse, but it will not affect the scope of this article as far as the Church is concerned.

Other Anglican churches, including those of Wales, Scotland and Ireland, are already separate from the state, and so the provisions of this article do not apply to them, though the principles that govern the relations between the spiritual and the secular spheres in England are generally followed by these other churches insofar as they can be. Anglicans believe that the Church must minister to the nation, including the state authorities, but that their spheres of competence are different and that there is no place for the kind of theocracy that until recently was common in both Roman Catholic and Eastern Orthodox countries.

The local articles may be summarized as follows:

1. Each local (national) church is free to order its internal affairs as it sees fit in matters that do not touch on fundamental Christian doctrine.

2. The Church of England has set forms of doctrinal preaching and of ordination that it uses to convey biblical teaching to its members.

3. Church and state are in relationship to one another but have distinct roles in society, and each must operate according to its own internal principles.

▪ 5 ▪

Miscellaneous Provisions

(Articles 38–39)

T he last two articles do not fit easily into what has gone before. They are of universal application but are not really part of the catholic faith as defined in Articles 1–8, nor do they concern the way of salvation or the doctrines of the church, ministry, and the sacraments. Their position at the end of the Articles corresponds to the way in which certain miscellaneous items are placed at the end of the Apostles' and Nicene Creeds, though the subjects treated are not the same.

ARTICLE 38: OF CHRISTIAN MEN'S GOODS, WHICH ARE NOT COMMON

> The Riches and Goods of Christians are not common, as touching the right, title, and possession of the same, as certain Anabaptists do falsely boast. Notwithstanding, every man ought, of such things as he possesseth, liberally to give alms to the poor, according to his ability.

This article rejects the primitive communism that was practiced by many early Anabaptists and accepts the legitimacy of private property. At the same time, it also advocates charitable giving as a Christian duty. In modern times this has often turned into support for high taxation to fund the welfare state, but although some Anglicans have decried this as creeping socialism, the Church has never advocated the confiscation of property or the forced redistribution of wealth. Social justice remains a desired goal for most Anglicans, but the Church believes that it must be obtained by means that respect the freedom and conscience of individuals, who should be persuaded that policies with that aim in view are right in themselves.

Charitable giving has always been close to the heart of Anglican piety, and it continues to be so today. Anglicans sometimes establish their own welfare organizations or cooperate with other Christian bodies in doing so, but Church members are encouraged to give to a wide range of causes. Occasionally, preference is given to Anglicans or other Christians (in allocating places in Church schools, for example), but this is not a matter of principle, and Anglicans usually come to the aid of anyone who is in need, regardless of his or her personal faith (or lack thereof). There has never been any suggestion that the recipients of Church aid should be required to profess some degree of Christian faith or belong to the Church, and coercion of that kind is generally deplored by Anglicans.

Article 39: Of a Christian Man's Oath

> As we confess that vain and rash Swearing is fora
> bidden Christian men by our Lord Jesus Christ,
> and *James* his Apostle, so we judge, that Christian
> Religion doth not prohibit, but that a man may
> swear when the Magistrate requireth, in a cause
> of faith and charity, so it be done according to the
> Prophet's teaching, in justice, judgement, and truth.

The article allows that it is lawful for Christians to take oaths in a court of law or in other legal situations (like signing a contract, for example). There was confusion in the sixteenth century between this kind of oath-taking and popular swearing, or cursing, which was universally condemned, as it is here. In the middle ages, monks and clergy often claimed to be exempt from the need to swear oaths because they assumed that their status would guarantee their honesty. That idea was taken over by some radical Protestants, who also refused to swear legal oaths for the same reason. Anglicans do not deny that some people are honest and that their word can be trusted, but they also recognize that we live in a fallen world and that people must be held to account, as long as this is done in a legally defensible way. The prophet referred to is Jeremiah, who said, "If you swear 'As the LORD lives,' in truth, in justice, and in righteousness, then nations shall bless themselves in him, and in him shall they glory" (Jer 4:2).

Christians are called to exercise their freedom responsibly and to accept that they must operate according to the laws of a world in which it is necessary to restrain the sinful proclivities of all human beings, including believers.

Transparency before the law is the right approach, and no one can be allowed to claim exemption from it on the basis of faith or Church membership. Honesty is the best policy, but it cannot always be taken for granted, even among Christians, and for that reason the Church allows that proper precautions may be taken by the appropriate lawful authorities.

The miscellaneous Articles may be summed up as follows:

1. Christians must be generous towards the poor and use their resources to demonstrate God's love for others.

2. Christians must be honest, upright, and trustworthy citizens and act according to the law as far as their conscience allows.

▪ 6 ▪

The Book of Common Prayer

It is notable that, in their present form, the Thirty-nine Articles say nothing about the *Book of Common Prayer*, which many Anglicans claim is a source of Anglican doctrine. Given that both the *Homilies* and the Ordinal are mentioned in the Articles, this omission may have been accidental, but if so, it reflects the fact that the Prayer Book was not as central to the Church's theology as many have thought.

One of the difficulties with the Prayer Book is that for doctrinal purposes it is usually referred to in the singular, whereas in practice there are many different books. Until recently, they had a strong family resemblance, but in the past generation a renewed interest in liturgy has changed all that. Anglicanism can still be characterised as "Prayer Book religion," but only if it is accepted that the content of the Prayer Book may be quite different from one Anglican Church to another.

Historically, and until the mid-nineteenth century, there was only a single Prayer Book tradition, though it had two branches that did not always overlap. The first Prayer Book was issued in 1549 and remained in use for just over three years. It was the first comprehensive English-language liturgy and contained a number of features that can be regarded as holdovers from medieval times. These are especially evident in the service of Holy Communion, which has always been the main focus of attention in the different Prayer Books.

The first Prayer Book was replaced by a second one in 1552, but it survived in official use for only a year. It was suppressed under Queen Mary I (1553–1558) but reissued in a revised version in 1559. The 1552 Book is more radical than its predecessor, especially in the rite for Holy Communion, where the ambiguities of 1549 that allowed some people to use the new book without abandoning the doctrine of transubstantiation were explicitly excluded. The 1559 Book was essentially that of 1552, with a few concessions to the more conservative 1549 one.

The 1552/1559 tradition was renewed in 1604, with the issuing of a slightly revised Book (which included a catechism for the first time), and again in 1662, after which it became the classical Anglican liturgy. The 1549 tradition resurfaced in 1636, when a "high church" Scottish Prayer Book was issued. The majority of Scots rejected it, but a minority clung to it. Representatives of that minority, constituted after 1690 in the Scottish Episcopal Church, ordained the first American bishop, which may account for its influence in shaping the American Prayer Book of 1786.

In the nineteenth century, there were a number of new editions of the Prayer Book, especially in the "settler" dominions of Canada and Australia, as well as in some other former colonial churches. For the most part, these were little more than adaptations of 1662 to different local contexts. However, the renewal of interest in liturgy that swept across the Christian world in the twentieth century had a major impact on Anglicanism that has transformed the scene entirely.

The 1662 *Book of Common Prayer* remains the official liturgy of the Church of England, and it is still widely used (often in translation) in Africa and Asia. Elsewhere, the traditional Prayer Book has been replaced by a wide variety of worship styles reflecting historical, indigenous, and/or modern theological trends of various kinds. Nevertheless, it retains its place of honor as the classical Anglican liturgy for the worldwide Anglican Communion, and if any Prayer Book is to be used for establishing Anglican doctrine, it can only be that one. It is therefore encouraging to see that very recently, editions of the 1662 Book have been prepared with a view toward reaching the worldwide Anglican Communion. These editions omit the state prayers, which pertain only to the United Kingdom and Commonwealth countries that recognize Queen Elizabeth II as their sovereign (notably Canada, Australia, and New Zealand), update some archaic language, and add occasional prayers to supplement those found in the 1662 Book.

PRELIMINARIES

The Book begins with two prefaces, one composed in 1662 and the other in 1549. The second is basically a fuller exposition of Article 34 on the permissible variations of tradition, whereas the first is an explanation of how the liturgy is intended to be a balance between complete freedom of worship (which was thought to be conducive to anarchy) and total rigidity (which might have been accused of quenching the Spirit). It must be said, however, that a significant number of English clergymen rejected the 1662 Book because it was too rigid and traditionalist for their liking, and they left the Church of England to form what would become the dissenting, or non-conformist, tradition that now includes Baptists, Presbyterians, Methodists, and other non-Anglican Protestants, though not Lutherans (who were not native to England).

After the prefaces come tables for the regular reading of Scripture, including the monthly cycle of Psalms. This lectionary, as it is called, has been revised several times. The two forms of the lectionary included in the 1662 Book, the second of which dates only from 1922, are seldom used nowadays. The main point of controversy surrounding them is the inclusion of readings from the Apocrypha. These were mandated in 1662 but made optional in 1922, and it is the second pattern that usually prevails today.

DAILY PRAYERS

The 1662 Book provides for Morning and Evening Prayer (sometimes called Mattins and Evensong) that are meant to be said or sung throughout the year. Appended to these are the Athanasian Creed, the Litany, and Prayers and Thanksgivings for special occasions. The emphasis is on the need for repentance as a preliminary to approaching God in worship. This is followed by the reading of the psalms set for the day, as well as portions of both the Old and New Testaments. The Bible readings are followed by canticles, most of which are taken from Scripture. The exceptions are the *Te Deum Laudamus* and the *Benedicite*, both of which are set for reading after the Old Testament lesson at Morning Prayer. In each case, there is an alternative canticle provided, and custom has determined that the second ones are generally used in Advent and Lent, though that is not explicitly required.

The Athanasian Creed is appointed to be read thirteen times in the year on dates chosen because they are spaced out at roughly a month's interval. The Litany was once used to transition from Morning Prayer to Holy Communion, but that practice has fallen into disuse in most places, and it is only seldom heard nowadays. The special Prayers and Thanksgivings mainly concern prayers for the weather, for peace, for the avoidance of epidemics, and for the legislature. Prayers for the royal family are included in both Morning and Evening Prayer, where they play an exceptionally large part, reflecting the origin and established status of the Church of England.

HOLY COMMUNION

After the daily prayers comes an extended section devoted to the sacrament of Holy Communion, which liturgists have always focused on as central to the Church's worship, though it was only in the mid-twentieth century that its celebration became a regular weekly event and often the main (or only) service on most Sundays.

The liturgy itself is preceded by a set of "collects" (emphasis on the first syllable), accompanied by a reading from one of the Epistles and one of the Gospels for every Sunday and major holy day throughout the year. This follows the ancient pre-Reformation pattern and is used in conjunction with Holy Communion. Alternative Scripture readings are often provided nowadays, but the traditional collects are still widely used and offer a model for other prayers.

The rite of Holy Communion itself begins with the Lord's Prayer, followed by a collect for purity of heart and mind and a summons to repentance based on the Ten Commandments. After that come two prayers for the monarch, of which one is chosen for use, and that is followed by the collect, Epistle, and Gospel readings for the day.

The Scripture readings are then followed by the Nicene Creed, which is meant to act as a kind of filter for the interpretation of Scripture. After that there is a brief pause for notices, followed by the sermon. The positioning here is significant, because it illustrates how the sermon is supposed to expound the Bible in the light of the Nicene Creed.

After the sermon comes the Offertory, when the people present their alms (the "collection") while the celebrant prepares the Table for the Supper. Once that is ready, the congregation prays a general prayer for the state of the church "militant here in earth." This is followed by three Exhortations, none of which is in common use today, but each of which tells us something important about the celebration.

The first Exhortation is meant to be used when the minister announces his intention to celebrate Holy Communion on the following Sunday or holy day. Now that celebrations are much more frequent than they used to be, this Exhortation is largely redundant, but it reminds us of the solemnity of the occasion, something that over-familiarity with the rite may encourage people to forget.

The second Exhortation was meant to be used when it was clear that congregants were not coming to Communion. Again, that is unusual nowadays because most people who attend regular worship communicate as a matter of course, but it serves to remind us that the sacrament is important and ought to figure prominently in the devotional life of every church member.

It is the third Exhortation, meant to be read at the time of the communion itself, that retains its significance, because it is a reminder of the need for self-examination before coming to Communion and warns those present that they must repent and amend their lives before doing so. Unfortunately, the significance of this is often lost on modern congregations because this prayer is almost always omitted, a mistake that distorts the true meaning of what then follows.

The Exhortations give way to a brief Invitation, followed by a lengthier Confession that is said by the entire congregation. The celebrant, who must be a presbyter, then pronounces Absolution of all those who are truly penitent and recites the Comfortable Words that are taken from the New Testament and intended to reassure us that those who repent are forgiven and encouraged to trust in Christ as their only mediator before God.

Next, we are directed to turn our attention to the Lord's Table and join in a prayer of Thanksgiving for the life, death, and resurrection of Jesus Christ. After that comes the Prayer of Humble Access, which was introduced at the Reformation and was not part of the ancient liturgies. In it we confess our complete unworthiness to stand in the presence of God and our complete trust in his mercy, which he has poured out to us in the atoning sacrifice of his Son. Next comes the Prayer of Consecration, in which it is made plain that the service is not repeating the sacrifice of Christ but rather remembering what he has done for us on the cross, something that he himself commanded his disciples to do.

As soon as the prayer of Consecration is finished, the communicants approach the table and kneel to receive first the bread and then the cup of wine. The words of administration used by the celebrant combine those of 1549 and 1552, reminding us of how the two original rites differ and how they have been reconciled. The 1549 words are more objective and could easily be translations of Latin, whereas the 1552 ones are subjective and more clearly English in flavor:

1549:	1552:
The body of our Lord Jesus Christ which was given for thee, preserve thy body and soul unto everlasting life.	Take and eat this in remembrance that Christ died for thee, and feed on him in thy heart by faith with thanksgiving.
The blood of our Lord Jesus Christ which was shed for thee, preserve thy body and soul unto everlasting life.	Drink this, in remembrance that Christ died for thee, and be thankful.

The 1549 words can be readily Latinized as follows: *Corpus (sanguis) Domini nostri Iesu Christi, quod (qui) datum (datus) est pro te, conservet corpus tuum et animam tuam in vitam aeternam.* But the 1552 words are less Latinate in form. "Take and eat this" would be bad Latin if translated literally, because Latin would prefer to say, "Take this and eat (it)," putting a direct object after each verb. It is a subtle point but one that faithfully reflects the desire of the Reformers to challenge communicants directly and in their own language.

After the Communion, the service ends with the Lord's Prayer, followed by a collective Thanksgiving that once more emphasizes that we have been justified before God on the basis of our faith alone. Finally, we conclude with a song of praise (the Gloria) and the parting Blessing, sometimes referred to as the Benediction.

BAPTISM AND THE
OCCASIONAL OFFICES

The rest of the Prayer Book contains services for Baptism and the Occasional Offices, which are not in regular use but are reserved for special occasions in the life of the church and its members.

The main baptismal rite is designed for the baptism of infants. Until 1662, there was no official provision for adult baptism, but overseas missionary expansion reminded the Church that it would sometimes be necessary, and so a service for it was added. This pattern reflects sixteenth- and seventeenth-century reality rather than theological propriety. Nowadays, everyone would agree that adult baptism is primary and infant baptism an adaptation of it, not the other way around.

The rites of infant baptism (one for public and the other for private baptisms) focus on the faith of the parents and godparents, who are reminded that they must bring the child up in the knowledge and fear of the Lord. Controversy has arisen over the prayer that follows the baptism, and this for two reasons. First, there is the signing with the cross (on the infant's forehead), with the words "in token that hereafter he shall not be ashamed to confess the faith of Christ crucified." The Puritans objected to this because to them it smacked of ritualistic magic, and its inclusion in 1662 was one of the reasons why so many of them left the Church. Today, however, few people would notice this or be bothered by it, and in a world where persecution has once more become a reality for many Christians, the call to fight under Christ's banner until our life's end resonates more than it once did.

The more modern controversy concerns the next line, which reads, "Seeing now ... that this child is regenerate and grafted into the body of Christ's Church … " Some have read this as an affirmation of baptismal regeneration, but that interpretation was quashed in the Gorham Judgment of 1850, when Charles Gorham, who rejected baptismal regeneration, was vindicated against the bishop of Exeter, who did and who wanted to insist on it. The Gorham Judgment led some Anglo-Catholics to leave the Church for Roman Catholicism, which affirms baptismal regeneration, but it set Anglicans free to preach the gospel even to those who had been baptized. The logic is that all baptized infants have been promised an inheritance in Christ but that they must claim it for themselves at whatever age they come to understand it.

After the rites of baptism comes the Catechism (added in 1604 but composed a generation earlier), which is designed to teach children the content of the Christian faith and to prepare them for Confirmation, which follows next. Then comes a rite for the solemnization of matrimony, which is explicitly restricted to one man and one woman, followed by a series of three: the visitation of the sick, the communion of the sick, and the burial of the dead. Finally, there are two other services, one for thanksgiving after childbirth, popularly called the "Churching of Women," and the other a Commination, or denouncing of God's wrath against sinners, a somewhat odd service (from the modern perspective) that is meant to be used mainly on Ash Wednesday. Its main purpose is to remind the church that spiritual discipline is necessary and that it is best exercised when individual church members are challenged to submit to it voluntarily, without being forced to do so by any outside authority. Nowadays, of course, no church has the power to discipline its members in the way that was common in the sixteenth century, but that makes the exhortation even more necessary, since it is only by voluntary submission that it will take place.

CONCLUSION

These rites form the bulk of the *Book of Common Prayer*, and they are often supplemented by special thanksgivings and so on. The prayers are followed by the complete Psalter, in the 1535 translation of Miles Coverdale, which in turn gives way to forms of prayer to be used at sea, which for obvious reasons are seldom heard by ordinary churchgoers. The Ordinal is then appended to the Book, as is a form to be used for the commemoration of the monarch's accession (currently on 6 February), and finally the Thirty-nine Articles. These are not part of the Prayer Book itself but accompany it as a reminder of the confession of faith to which Anglicans are committed.

As stated above, there is now a wide variety of Prayer Books across the Anglican Communion, including a number of Alternative Services authorized for use in the Church of England. Some Anglicans might appeal to one or more of these on the mistaken impression that any Prayer Book can be used as indicative of the Church's doctrine, but such an appeal would receive no official backing and would almost certainly be dismissed if presented as evidence in a court of law.

• 7 •

Church Government (Ecclesiology)

Anglicanism is distinguished from other Christian traditions by its ecclesiology. It uniquely combines Catholic and Protestant elements. To some outside observers this is a sign of confusion; they would prefer what to them would be a more consistently Catholic or Protestant pattern. Others, however, see in Anglicanism a blending of influences that does justice to the full range of Christian ecclesiology and offers a model that might one day help to reunite a divided Christendom. For the moment, the most useful thing we can do is to outline the principles that underlie Anglican ecclesiological doctrine and the practice of church government, so that the wider ecumenical discussion can proceed on the basis of a clear understanding of what the Anglican approach actually is.

THE CHURCH

Anglicans believe that they form part of the "Church of God," an expression used to mean the entire body of orthodox Christians, regardless of denomination. There may be some dispute about which other churches belong to this universal "Church of God," but on the whole, any regularly constituted Trinitarian body is recognized by most Anglicans as coming within this umbrella description.

In practice, this means that anyone baptized in a Trinitarian church, and a regular communicant thereof, is welcome to receive communion in an Anglican church. Some very high-church Anglicans dispute this, but they are very much a minority nowadays. Similarly, Anglicans recognize the baptisms of other Trinitarian churches and do not demand that their members should be rebaptized if they wish to become Anglicans. People joining an Anglican church may be asked to submit to Confirmation, especially if they come from a non-episcopal body, but this is a formality and does not affect their right to communicate in an Anglican setting.

More complex is the question of the recognition of orders granted by other churches. In general, clergy coming from other episcopal churches are welcomed without hesitation, whereas those who come from a non-episcopal church may have to be re-ordained. Here the situation is evolving towards greater recognition of the non-episcopally ordained, but there is still a considerable variety among the different churches of the Anglican Communion, and it is too soon to speak of a common policy on this subject. Individual Anglican Churches are not required to recognize Anglican orders conferred elsewhere, and some impose special qualifications on those who are ordained in one Anglican Church but wish to minister in another. This underscores the autonomy of local Anglican Churches and weakens the sense of the Church's overall catholicity, but the fact that individual churches may have mutually incompatible criteria for ordination makes it inevitable, and the situation is unlikely to change in the foreseeable future.

Is it possible to be Anglican without being in communion with the archbishop (or more correctly, with the see) of Canterbury? The Anglican Communion recognizes the archbishop of Canterbury as its titular head, but he is not to be compared with the pope. In many respects he is closer to the patriarch of Constantinople in the Eastern Orthodox Church. He is "first among equals" but has no jurisdiction outside his own province and cannot intervene in any other Anglican body unless he is invited to do so.

The question arises because there are churches that purport to be Anglican but that are not recognized by Canterbury, although most of them would like to be. For instance, the Anglican Church of North America (ACNA) is not a member of the Anglican Communion, but it is recognized by several churches that are. This can create an awkward situation—for example, if the churches that recognize ACNA refuse to attend gatherings called by Canterbury unless Canterbury also recognizes it. At the present time, there is a real conflict of opposing recognitions of this kind that has not been resolved, but that calls into question the importance of Canterbury as a link between Anglicans.

A different kind of question arises from relations between individual Anglican churches and non-Anglican bodies. For example, the Church of England is in communion with the Scandinavian Lutheran churches, but this does not extend to the Anglican Communion as a whole. As a result, a Lutheran minister from Iceland may be free to work in England but not necessarily in Uganda or Australia. The result is an anomalous situation that may be regarded as theologically incoherent but is difficult to resolve for administrative and jurisdictional reasons.

THE MINISTRY

All Anglican churches have bishops. Most (but not all) also have at least one archbishop who is the head of his ecclesiastical province. In addition, local Anglican Churches have a "primate" who is the nominal head of the Church as a whole. This is usually an archbishop, but the office may rotate among the senior clergy and in some cases be titled differently. In the United States, for example, the titular head of the Church is called the "presiding bishop" and is elected for a fixed nine-year term.

The head of the Church of England is the archbishop of Canterbury, who is the "primate of all England" and the presiding archbishop of the Anglican Communion, which is at least partially defined as being in communion with him.

Anglican bishops and archbishops are consecrated for life, though they may have to resign their particular ministry at a given age. Retired bishops retain their orders, however, and may continue to exercise them at the discretion of the local authorities.

The clergy are divided into presbyters (priests) and deacons. Deacons normally serve for six months to a year and are then ordained priests, though a permanent diaconate is possible. Most clergy are presbyters who are ordained for life but may have to retire at a certain age.

Clergy may renounce their orders and return to the lay state, but that is both rare and discouraged. As with bishops, retired presbyters and deacons may continue to function at the discretion of the local authorities.

Only bishops may confirm baptized persons or ordain clergy. Only bishops and presbyters may preside at Holy Communion. These regulations are for the order and good government of the Church, but they have no explicit biblical warrant and in theory could be changed. Often, lay people are licensed to perform certain tasks that are normally reserved for the ordained clergy, including preaching. These vary considerably from one place to another, but the principle is universal, and the practice is now widespread across the Anglican Communion.

There is a minimum age for ordination (twenty-three for the diaconate, twenty-four for the presbyterate, and thirty for the episcopate) but no maximum, though most clergy retire around the age of seventy or so, and it is unusual (though not unlawful) to ordain any lay person who is already of retirement age.

THE SACRAMENTS

Anyone may baptize, but usually it is the privilege of an ordained clergy person to do so. Lay baptism is possible but rather unusual, being reserved mainly for extreme cases, such as the emergency baptism of children who are expected to die shortly after birth. Baptism is normally by sprinkling, but there is no restriction on the mode, nor on the quantity of water that may be used.

In the case of infant baptism, the parents and godparents must make promises on the infant's behalf, but teenagers and adults are expected to respond for themselves. In the latter case, it would seem that Confirmation should be unnecessary, but it is still administered in practice.

The Lord's Supper (also called Holy Communion) is open to all Christians without restriction. The Church does not specify what kind of bread or wine should be used for the celebration, though it is assumed that whatever is chosen will be appropriate to the character and solemnity of the rite. Thus, for example, gluten-free wafers and unfermented grape juice would be fine, but doughnuts and coffee would not.

No restrictions are placed on the number of times a person may communicate in one day. Traditionally, Anglicans have been encouraged to make their communion at Christmas, Easter and Pentecost (as a minimum) but it is not a requirement and is seldom mentioned nowadays. It is possible for a communicant to be present at the Lord's Supper without communicating, but such non-participation is usually a sign that the person concerned is experiencing some kind of spiritual difficulty, and abstention is not normally encouraged.

SYNODS

Synodical government is the norm in Anglican churches, but the nature of the synods and the patterns of their election vary from one local church to another. The universal principle is that bishops, clergy, and laity should all be represented and have an equal say in the government of the church. Most churches have a national synod that meets at periodic intervals, while there are also synods at provincial, diocesan, and deanery levels.[2] In addition, each congregation will have an annual church meeting at which officers are elected to serve for the coming year. The most important of these are the churchwardens, who must be laypeople and who are responsible for the upkeep of the parish church. Congregations usually elect a council, consisting of the minister, the wardens, and a number of elected representatives,

---

2. A province is the territory of an archbishop, consisting of several dioceses, each of which has its own bishop. A deanery is a subdivision of a diocese, presided over by a dean who is usually one of the local clergy. The United States is unusual, in that while both The Episcopal Church and the Reformed Episcopal Church have provinces, they do not have archbishops to preside over them.

who together run the day-to-day affairs of the congregation. The precise details vary from place to place, but the general principle is accepted by Anglicans everywhere. Voting rights and membership are usually set at a minimum of sixteen to eighteen years of age, but there is no generally imposed maximum.

CANON LAW

The Church of England inherited the medieval canon law, contained in what is known as the *Corpus Iuris Canonici*, which was supplemented by local English legislation, now collected in William Lyndwood's *Provinciale*, which was published in 1433. At the time of the Reformation, the Canon Law faculties at Oxford and Cambridge were abolished, and the intention was to reform the canons and integrate them into the common law. This did not happen, however, and today the Church of England is the only Christian body in which the medieval canons still have some authority, unless they have been superseded by subsequent legislation.

After the Reformation, there were several attempts to alter the canon law and to codify it on a new basis, but these failed. Instead, there was a series of canons passed at intervals during the reign of Elizabeth I (1558–1603), but the queen only ratified the last of these (in 1597). In 1604, a new set of canons was approved, and these became the "classical" ones, though that was as much by default as by design. In 1736, it was determined that since Parliament had not ratified these canons, they did not apply to the laity, which greatly restricted their scope. They were finally replaced in 1969, by which time they had almost gone out of use altogether.

Other Anglican churches have their own canons to regulate their government and worship, but in many cases their canon law is underdeveloped and still dependent on that of England, as far as setting a precedent is concerned. These churches may also possess ecclesiastical courts that seek to administer clergy discipline, but their scope and effectiveness varies widely across the Anglican Communion. As a state church, the Church of England possesses ecclesiastical courts that are officially recognized, but their jurisdiction is severely curtailed and ineffective beyond the bounds of the Church itself.

In recent years, there has been a great revival of interest in canon law among Anglicans, and attempts have been made to use it as a means of resolving conflicts over such matters as women's ordination and same-sex marriage. On the whole, it has to be said that these efforts have not been very successful, not least because the canons are no substitute for doctrine. Furthermore, they can easily be changed by legislation in order to reflect church practice, which is determined by the relevant synod(s). They can therefore be used to adjudicate disputes at any given moment, but not to determine principles of universal validity that lie beyond the law's competence. Rather like the *Book of Common Prayer*, the canon law reflects the doctrine of the Church but does not determine what it is (or ought to be).

Having said that, there is an active Anglican faculty of canon law at the University of Cardiff (Wales), an Ecclesiastical Law Society that holds regular conferences and publishes a serious academic journal, as well as a series of publications that debate questions of Anglican canon law and provide resources for canon lawyers who practice the discipline. How significant this is for the wider life of the Anglican Communion is hard to say, but it now seems very unlikely that Anglicanism will relapse into the state of semi-lawlessness that characterized some of its most important churches until quite recent times.

▪ 8 ▪

The Anglican World Today

Anglicanism as we know it today is a tradition with roots in the Reformation Church of England that has grown to become a global network of episcopally-ordered churches. These churches have a family resemblance to one another, even though it is hard to pin down in precise theological terms. The easiest way to describe their relationship is to think of it in terms of a series of concentric circles radiating out from Canterbury, whose archbishop is commonly regarded as its spiritual head because he is the highest ranking bishop in the Church of England.

The Church of England is an established state church, which means that its membership embraces the entire country, apart from those who have opted out of it. In practice, this means that Anglican ceremonies grace state occasions, in particular the coronation of the monarch, and that large numbers of people are baptized, married, and buried according to Anglican rites, even though they may never darken the door of a church. It also means that most English people claim the Church as part of their national heritage and many feel free to comment on its activities, even if they have no Christian belief at all.

Beyond the Church of England there is the Anglican Communion, a grouping of forty independent churches which can be classified according to the way they relate to the "mother Church." They can be grouped into eight cohorts—although one cohort of Anglican churches are not part of the Anglican Communion, though they are recognized by GAFCON (Global Anglican Futures Conference).

CHURCHES THAT WERE FORMERLY ESTABLISHED STATE CHURCHES IN THE BRITISH ISLES

This cohort includes the Church of Ireland (disestablished in 1869) and the Church in Wales (disestablished in 1920).

These Churches retain special links with the Church of England, particularly where their clergy are concerned. For example, an Irish or Welsh Anglican minister can move to the Church of England (and vice versa) without requiring special permission in the way that "overseas" clergy do. The Irish Church has a strong evangelical element, especially in Northern Ireland, whereas the Welsh Church is mainly liberal Anglo-Catholic in orientation. Within this grouping would also be included the Anglican Church in various British Overseas Territories like Bermuda and the Falkland Islands, where a colonial establishment still exists.

REBEL CHURCHES

This cohort includes the Episcopal Church of Scotland (from 1690) and the Episcopal Church of the United States (from 1786).

These Churches owe their origins to political events. In Scotland, Episcopalianism was overthrown during the Glorious Revolution of 1688–1689 and replaced by Presbyterianism. For some years in the eighteenth century, the Scottish Episcopal Church was illegal, and the Church of England maintained extra-territorial parishes in Scotland where Anglicans could worship. The last of these was not integrated into the Scottish Episcopal Church until 1987. In the United States, the American Revolution broke the links with the British Crown and obliged members of the Church of England to set up a new denomination, which in its early years did its best to distance itself from England. Not only did it modify the Articles of Religion, but it also produced a new Prayer Book and refused to have archbishops presiding over it. This last feature is now an anomaly in the Anglican world, but it seems likely to continue for the foreseeable future. Out of the missionary work of the American Episcopal Church several other Churches have emerged: the Anglican Church of the Central American Region, the Episcopal Anglican Church of Brazil, the Episcopal Church of Cuba, the Anglican Church of Mexico, and the Episcopal Church in the Philippines.

The American Episcopal Church also has overseas dioceses in places like Haiti, the Dominican Republic, Honduras, Venezuela, Colombia, Ecuador, Taiwan and Micronesia and a series of chaplaincies in continental Europe, alongside (but independent of) those of the Church of England.

SETTLER CHURCHES

This cohort includes the Anglican Church of Canada, the Anglican Church of Australia, the Anglican Church of Aotearoa, New Zealand and Polynesia, and the Anglican Church of Southern Africa.

These are Churches originally established by English settlers in former British colonies that still (by and large) reflect that origin. The New Zealand Church is subdivided into three divisions (called *tikanga*) along ethnic lines.

There is a White (Pakeha) Church, a Maori Church, and a Polynesian Church, which covers a large part of the South Pacific. There has also been considerable missionary work in southern Africa, where the European membership of the Church is now a minority. Like the Church of England, these settler churches are mixed bodies, with evangelical, Anglo-Catholic, and Broad church elements in varying degrees.

COLONIAL MISSIONARY CHURCHES

This cohort includes the Anglican Church of Papua New Guinea, the Church of the Province of Melanesia, the Church of the Province of Central Africa, the Church of the Province of the Indian Ocean, the Anglican Church of Kenya, the Anglican Church of Tanzania, the Church of the Province of Uganda, the Church of the Province of the Sudan, the Church of Nigeria, the Church of the Province of West Africa, the Province of the Anglican Church in South East Asia, Hong Kong Sheng Kung Hui, the Church of the Province of Myanmar (Burma), and the Church in the Province of the West Indies

These Churches are remnants of the former British Empire, though some have extended their mission into neighboring countries that were never under British rule. The ones outside Africa tend to be fairly high church in tone, as are the Churches of Central and West Africa. The Church of Tanzania is a combination of evangelical and Anglo-Catholic elements. The others are mainly evangelical and also of "colonial" origin, but they are outside the former Empire. These are the Anglican Church of the Southern Cone of America, the Anglican Church of Chile, the Anglican Church of the Province of Burundi, the Anglican Church of Rwanda, and the Church of the Province of Congo

These Churches originated in revival movements (in Africa) and in mission work undertaken mainly by evangelicals, and they retain a strongly conservative and evangelical flavor.

NON-COLONIAL MISSIONARY CHURCHES

This cohort includes the Anglican Church in Korea, the Anglican Communion in Japan, and the Episcopal Church in Jerusalem and the Middle East , and the Church of Alexandria (Egypt). The Churches in Korea and Japan are fairly high church in orientation, but the Church in Jerusalem and the Middle East is mainly evangelical, as is the Church of Alexandria (Egypt).

FORMER "COLONIAL" CHURCHES NOW UNITED WITH OTHER DENOMINATIONS

This cohort includes the Church of North India, the Church of South India, the Church of Pakistan, the Church of Ceylon (Sri Lanka), and the Church of Bangladesh. These Churches are somewhat mixed in terms of churchmanship, though the fact that they are pan-Protestant means that a low or basically evangelical element tends to predominate.

ASSOCIATE CHURCHES

This cohort includes the Lusitanian Church (Portugal) and the Spanish Episcopal Reformed Church. These churches were established partly by Anglican missionaries and partly by local Roman Catholics who dissented from the declaration of papal infallibility in 1870. They are both officially Anglican now, but their links with the rest of the Anglican world are fairly tenuous. It is hard to classify them in terms of churchmanship, but "non-papal Catholic" is perhaps the best description of what they are like.

EPISCOPAL CHURCHES OUTSIDE THE ANGLICAN COMMUNION

This cohort includes the Free Church of England, the Reformed Episcopal Anglican Church (REACH) in South Africa, the Reformed Episcopal Church (in the United States), and the Anglican Church of North America (ACNA). The Reformed Episcopal Church is now part of the Anglican Church in North America, though so far it has retained a distinct identity. There are also several smaller Anglican Churches in the United States. The Free Church of England and REACH are evangelical, but the American ones are quite mixed in churchmanship terms.

THE OUTLOOK OF ANGLICANISM

What the future holds for the Anglican world is impossible to predict. Many of the churches listed here belong to GAFCON and/or to the Global South Network, both conservative groupings that resist the liberalizing tendencies present in the First World members of the Anglican Communion. Their aim is to purify those mixed Churches and return to a theologically orthodox and morally conservative fellowship of the kind that predominated until the 1970s. Where this has proved difficult or impossible (as in the United States), GAFCON and the Global South Network have recognized bodies like ACNA, which they hope will eventually displace the traditional Episcopal Church, unless (by some miracle) the latter returns to traditional orthodoxy.

It is that orthodoxy that unites evangelicals and Anglo-Catholics across traditional churchmanship divides, though the latter remain stronger among conservatives in the First World, making co-operation with GAFCON and the Global South more difficult. The basic problem is that while the churches of the developing world are relatively monochrome within themselves (though often quite different from each other), those of the First World are mixed bags, with no one element dominant or able to exclude the others. This, more than anything else, may produce different Anglicanisms by the end of the present century, though that remains to be seen. Whatever happens, Anglicanism is not static and is certain to look different in 2100 from the way it appears now, though at deeper levels it may still be much the same. Anglican churches may not be "always the same" (*semper eadem*), as the Roman Catholic Church likes to claim of itself, but it is very likely that "the more things change, the more they stay the same" (*plus ça change, plus c'est la même chose*). Quite what that will mean in practice, we shall have to wait and see.

Index

What is ANGLICANISM?

Many associations come to mind. Whether the buildings, unique history, prayers, or church government, we often emphasize one aspect of Anglicanism over the others. Is the Anglican church a Protestant church with distinctive characteristics, or a Catholic Church no longer in communion with Rome?

In *Anglicanism: A Reformed Catholic Tradition*, Gerald Bray argues that some theological trajectories are more faithful than others to the nature and history of the Church of England. Readers looking to understand the diversity, nature, and future of Anglicanism will be helped by Bray's historical examination.

◆

"Gerald Bray writes in the spirit of J. I. Packer and John Stott and has gifted the church with an unrivaled brief introduction to Anglicanism. *Deo gratias!*"

MARK BOWALD
professor of theology, Grace Theological Seminary

◆

GERALD BRAY is research professor of divinity at Beeson Divinity School of Samford University (Birmingham, Alabama). He is the author of numerous books, including *Preaching the Word with John Chrysostom, God Has Spoken*, and *Doing Theology with the Reformers*.

RELIGION / Christianity / Anglican

ISBN 978-1-68359-436-9

90000

US $23.99

LEXHAM PRESS
lexhampress.com

9 781683 594369